THIS JOURNAL
BELONGS TO

_____

_____

_____

THE
100-DAY
FINANCIAL
GOAL
JOURNAL

**BUILD A PLAN
FOR YOUR
FINANCIAL FUTURE**

ALYSSA DAVIES

STERLING
New York

STERLING
New York

An Imprint of Sterling Publishing Co., Inc.
1166 Avenue of the Americas
New York, NY 10036

ISBN 978-1-4549-3998-6

Distributed in Canada by Sterling Publishing Co., Inc.
℅ Canadian Manda Group, 664 Annette Street
Toronto, Ontario M6S 2C8, Canada
Distributed in the United Kingdom by GMC Distribution Services
Castle Place, 166 High Street, Lewes, East Sussex BN7 1XU, England
Distributed in Australia by NewSouth Books
University of New South Wales, Sydney, NSW 2052, Australia

For information about custom editions, special sales, and
premium and corporate purchases, please contact Sterling Special Sales
at 800-805-5489 or specialsales@sterlingpublishing.com.

Manufactured in Singapore

2 4 6 8 10 9 7 5 3 1

sterlingpublishing.com

Cover design by Igor Satanovsky
Interior design by Christine Heun

INTRODUCTION

Have you ever felt completely disconnected from your money? Sure, you earn it, you spend it, and you attempt to save it—but what about making a plan with it? How do you set and reach a financial goal? If you picked up this journal because you like money, wish you had more of it, and want to learn the answers to these questions, you've come to the right place. This guided daily journal is here to help you set an achievable financial goal that can be accomplished in 100 days, whether you want to save for a financial emergency, pay off your credit cards, or run off to Hawaii for the summer. Along the way, you'll learn about your money habits and patterns, track your spending and saving, and develop a game plan that suits your budget and lifestyle. (Because yes, you'll actually have to make a budget!) You'll turn your financial stress into financial success by learning how to take care of your money and reflecting on how you spend each day.

Think of this journal as a safe haven for those of us looking for an honest and free place to think about your financial goals and to learn how to manage your money. While a lot of financial advice preaches that you cut back on non-essential spending and tighten up those purse strings, this journal won't tell you to stop spending money on things that make you happy. After all, isn't that why we set financial goals? There are no rules that dictate the best ways to organize your life and fulfill your needs or judgments about what you consider a financial need.

For anyone who wants to take control of their finances, it can be seriously overwhelming to find a starting point, but personal finance doesn't have to be intimidating. The good news about your financial habits is that you are ready to grow and change; otherwise, you wouldn't have picked up this journal. That's step one. And you're already doing so well!

HOW TO USE THIS JOURNAL

Most personal finance tools and journals are strictly focused on tracking all of your spending or budgeting. While these are important, you also need to stay on track psychologically. Saving money requires discipline and willpower. Both of these traits come with some behavioral challenges that will, at times, make it difficult to avoid spending on non-essential items. Spending money is emotional. Some of us shop to escape a bad day, while others shop for the instant gratification that is to own something new. This journal can help you swap out "retail therapy" for self-reflection and a deeper understanding of your money.

At the beginning of each week, you'll find a Weekly Focus, followed by seven Connect & Reflect pages and one Weekly Outlook page. Each week begins with a Weekly Focus section, which will offer an important financial lesson and some actionable prompts and questions that will help you take control of your money.

On the Connect & Reflect pages of this journal, you will track your mood and how your money makes you feel each day. Money and your mood go hand in hand. If you end your day and find that you are feeling down, it's a great time to acknowledge that this feeling may spill over into your financial success for the following day. You also have room to assess your current financial situation, explore how you want your money to work for you, and take note of some particular challenges and successes that you faced that day. Are things going well? Does money currently stress you out? These pages offer you the space you need to think about those questions.

Next up, you will complete the Weekly Outlook pages. The purpose of these pages is to manifest your financial success. Manifestation is the act of saying something aloud or doing something to reflect an idea or image that you desire, but that has yet to happen. In other words, you are attempting to take a vision and turn it into reality by simply voicing and believing that it will happen. You will focus on how you can improve your financial habits, recognize your best decision of the previous week, and provide yourself with the motivation you need for the upcoming week. You'll also set affirmations—true statements with a positive connotation—for the next week. Think of your affirmations as assured self-encouragement.

Remember, money can be exhausting. It's okay to have a hard week, and it's okay to feel success. You're doing everything right—even if it feels wrong. There are no wrong answers for the questions on the Connect & Reflect or Weekly Outlook pages.

DAY 84

Date 5/5

CONNECT & REFLECT

Current mood (circle one):

I FEEL happy to finally take control of my financial situation rather than let it control me.

MONEY IS CURRENTLY the least stressful part of my day!

I WANT MONEY TO be something that is always in abundance so that I don't need to worry about how I will pay for upcoming bills or plans.

WHAT WERE CHALLENGES THAT I FACED TODAY?
1. My co-worker wanted to go for lunch today and wouldn't take no for an answer.
2. I had a personal appointment after work and parking was $19.
3. The decision to leave my all-friends group chat because planning expensive trips are currently not a financial goal for me.

WHAT ARE SUCCESSES THAT I ENJOYED TODAY?
1. My co-worker agreed to pay for my lunch! Woo!
2. I made dinner at home—which is a big deal for me.
3. My friends understood when I told them I couldn't attend the trip they planned.

WHERE DO I STAND?

☐ I need to get back on track to achieve my financial goal.

☑ I am on track with my financial goal.

TODAY'S EXPENSES

BUDGET CATEGORY	ITEM	COST
Entertainment	Movie Night	$13.48
TOTAL		$13.48

TODAY'S INCOME

ITEM	AMOUNT
Full-time job (Payday)	$1,500
TOTAL	$1,500

WEEKLY OUTLOOK

What could you improve on financially this week?

I could do a better job of saying no to expensive nights out
with friends. Last night, I went to dinner, which ended up
turning into an expensive pub crawl. If I had stayed in or
asked them to come over for dinner instead, I could've saved
upward of $200.

What was the best financial decision you made last week?

I showed my partner how I budget, and now they want to do
the same!

Next week's motivations:

1. I want to be able to support myself without help from family.

2. I want to feel confident in myself.

3. I no longer want to feel the need to compare myself to my
friends.

I WILL be patient with myself and with my money.

_____

_____

_____

I WILL NOT spend any money on takeout food.

_____

_____

I AM going to buy myself a coffee on Friday morning as a
treat for making it through the week.

_____

LAST PURCHASE: rent

_____

COST: $800

_____

THIS WEEK'S SAVINGS: $100

TOTAL MONEY SAVED/DEBT REPAID SO FAR: _____

_____

CURRENT WANT(S): Bottle of wine, new shoes, and tickets
for a music festival this weekend.

CURRENT NEED(S): Groceries, a night in to regroup and relax

_____

ASSESS YOUR FINANCIAL LIFE

Before you can set a financial goal, you need to know where you stand with your current situation. Estimates aren't going to get you to the finish line. You need to know where every cent that hits your bank account comes from and where it goes. A solid financial assessment doesn't come without taking a long, hard look at what you earn and how much you spend. Plus, you can use this information to determine whether your financial goal should focus on saving for the future or repaying debts owed.

There are a couple of different ways to analyze your current financial situation. First, you can look at your net worth. Typically, the goal with money is to increase your overall net worth over time. To calculate your net worth, you should subtract any liabilities from assets you owe. An asset is something of value, such as your savings, your home, or your estate. A liability would be anything considered to be debt, such as a student loan or credit card bill.

Another comfortable place to start is to write down all your monthly expenses and income to see how much you spend every single month. Rather than put all of these numbers into a spreadsheet, it's always beneficial to write them out by hand to fully digest the reality of your current financial situation.

You can also start by doing a deep dive into the debts you currently owe. If you have credit card debt, student loans, or a vehicle payment, you should at the very minimum be aware of how much money you need to put toward these repayments. Try not to take on any more debt until you have paid off what you currently owe. Also look at your options for the best way to tackle debt. Perhaps you should consolidate all of your debt into one payment through a credit counseling agency. Maybe you want to repay the debt that has the highest interest rate first. If you feel as though your interest is making it impossible to pay the balance owed, contact the company that holds your loan and do some negotiating.

Ultimately, you want to ensure that you aren't spending more than you're bringing in. A common point of contention for many people trying to get their finances under control is the fact that they live outside of their means. If you spend too much money, it becomes impossible to save and also very hard to avoid debt.

ASSETS

Savings:

1. _____
2. _____
3. _____
4. _____
5. _____
6. _____
7. _____
8. _____
9. _____
10. _____

PROPERTY

1. Home Value _____
2. Other Land/Property _____
3. Vehicle _____
4. Valuables (Art, Collectibles, etc.) _____

TOTAL _____

LIABILITIES

1. Mortgage _____

2. Other mortgages _____

3. Credit cards _____

4. Vehicle Loan _____

5. Student Loan _____

6. Other debt(s) _____

TOTAL _____

ASSETS _____ minus **LIABILITIES** _____ =

NET WORTH _____

MONTHLY GROSS INCOME	AMOUNT
Wages/Salary	
Child/Spousal Maintenance	
Other Income	
TOTAL	

MONTHLY EXPENSES	COST
Mortgage or Rent	
Home/Fire Insurance Premiums	
Property Taxes	
Homeowner Association/Strata Fees	
Phone Bill	
Water & Sewer Bill	

Natural Gas Bill	
Internet/Cable TV/Streaming Subscriptions	
Food	
Household Incidentals	
Transportation/Vehicle Insurance	
Gasoline, Bus Fare, Parking	
Vehicle Loan/Lease Payment	
Personal Allowances (Entertainment, Beauty, Etc.)	
Prescription & Other Monthly Medical Expenses	
Health & Life Insurance Premiums	
Personal Loans	
Credit Card Payments	
Tithe, Charity, Foster Parent Plan & Donations	
Savings: Short-Term	
Savings: Long-Term	
Child or Spousal Support	
Child Care	
Pet Care	
TOTAL	

Monthly Net Income (monthly gross income minus expenses)	$

Are you living above your means?   ☐ Yes   ☐ No

CREATE A GOAL

It's time for the fun part: setting your financial goal. When you picked up this journal, you probably already knew exactly where you wanted to end up financially, but perhaps you can find a way to narrow that goal, make it more specific, and ensure that it's achievable based on your current financial situation.

FIND YOUR WHYS

To be successful with your financial goal, you'll need to have a purpose for pursuing it. Like following any passions in life, it can be overwhelming to try something new, but having a reason why you want to pursue this goal can help you stay motivated.

Writing down everything you've ever wanted in life is always a good exercise. Not only does it allow you to dream as big as you want, but it also allows you to get a broader look into the overarching themes behind your financial goal. If you consistently mention happiness or comfort, perhaps the motivation behind your financial goal is the ability to achieve financial independence.

LIST 10 OF YOUR CURRENT FINANCIAL GOALS OR GENERAL GOALS IN LIFE:

1. _____

2. _____

3. _____

4. _____

5. _____

6. _____

7. _____

8. _____

9. _____

10. _____

WHICH GOALS ARE THE MOST IMPORTANT TO YOU?

_____

_____

_____

_____

WHAT ARE THE OVERARCHING THEMES THAT YOU SEE IN YOUR MOST IMPORTANT GOALS?

_____

_____

_____

_____

_____

_____

Write a rough draft of your financial goal based on the themes listed below.

FIGURING OUT THE SPECIFICS

Most people set financial goals with the best of intentions, but they don't know how to make the goal realistic and purposeful. If your financial goal is too vague, you are setting yourself up for failure. Without a clear vision of where you see yourself and your money in a few months or a few years, you will struggle to stick to your goal during the hard parts of the always-challenging task of managing our money.

Goals should also be specific enough that you can measure your progress. You'll need to set a weekly savings goal and find a way to add additional income to that savings account. That means it's time to do some math. For example, if your financial goal requires you to save $1,000 in 100 days, this would mean you will need to save $10/day or roughly $70/week to accomplish your goal.

CAN YOU ANSWER YES TO THE FOLLOWING QUESTIONS?

☐ Can you explain this goal in less than three sentences and have a stranger understand it? If not, how can you make your goal easier to explain?

_____

_____

_____

☐ Is there a way to define the point you've reached the goal? In other words, how can you measure this goal?

_____

_____

_____

☐ Do you have the means and the income available to achieve this goal? If not, can you find a more workable number?

_____

_____

☐ Is this goal practical? Are you likely to succeed?

_____

_____

_____

HOW MUCH MONEY DOES YOUR GOAL REQUIRE YOU TO SAVE?

_____

DIVIDE THE GOAL BY 100

(the number of days you have to complete your goal).

How much will you need to save each day in order to achieve your goal by this deadline?

_____

Is this achievable?   ☐ Yes   ☐ No

If yes, you have determined your savings goal. If no, repeat the above task until you find a suitable savings goal.

Who can you talk to about your financial situation, or what apps could you use?

1. _____

2. _____

3. _____

Would you trust this person or app to help hold you accountable?

☐ Yes   ☐ No

If you do not feel comfortable finding an accountability buddy or using an app, try a weekly phone reminder. Put this reminder into your phone and keep it set to repeat until you accomplish your goal.

MAKE A COMMITMENT

Just like any new adventure we begin, it doesn't truly count until we make an official commitment. Start at a new gym? Sign a contract and make a payment. Join a sports team? Sign a waiver and make a payment. Nothing changes here. If you write your goals down, it will set the tone that you need to finally take control of your money and do things you never thought possible. It's time to cross your T's and dot your I's. Once you have a financial goal, we will ensure that you will do everything in your power to hit your target and stay invested (pun intended).

The date you'd like to start your goal:

_____

The date you'd like to accomplish your goal:

_____

WRITE YOUR FINAL GOAL IN LESS THAN THREE SENTENCES:

_____

_____

_____

_____

_____

_____

_____

_____

YOUR LETTER OF COMMITMENT

Dear _____,

On this day of _____, I understand that my role as a human being who deeply cares for their financial future is a significant responsibility.

In this role, and through the duration of the journey to achieve my goal, I promise to:

☐ Always stay true to my "why"

☐ Fill out my journal and use these pages as an opportunity to focus on my goal

☐ Tackle every weekly focus within the journal with an open mind and the willingness to adjust

☐ Stick to my budget and pay attention to my finances on a weekly and monthly basis

☐ Hold myself accountable to all financial decisions I make from here on out

I have read and fully agree to this Letter of Commitment and look forward to accomplishing my financial goal and setting myself and my money up for success in the future.

DEADLINE: _____

SIGNATURE: _____

DATE: _____

PRINT NAME: _____

THIS WEEK'S FOCUS: BUDGET LIKE A CEO

THE WHAT

Budgeting will help you take control of your finances and ensure that you are doing everything in your power to achieve your goal. It's now time to choose what type of budget works best for you. If you already have a budget, it might be a good time to refresh or revise your plan. No matter what your situation is, it's vital that the method you want works best with your personality type and lifestyle.

THE WHY

The best way to organize and set your financial plans in motion is by building a budget that is suited to your lifestyle. Budgets help you prioritize your spending and determine where all of your money goes. If you have a budget, you don't have to guess whether you have enough money and will have a higher chance of completing your financial goal. If you wing it, the outcome might be as messy as your kitchen after a dinner party. Bottom line: organizing your finances is essential.

THE HOW

Once you feel like you understand your money and know how you want to control it, it's time to put that budget into practice. Whether it's a spreadsheet you adjust every couple of months or an app that updates daily, you must stick with it for a few weeks before changing to something new. It can take a while to get used to living with a budget, but it helps reduce stress on your wallet—and your mind.

WHAT ARE YOUR CURRENT FINANCIAL GOALS?
A) Debt repayment
B) Saving for short-term
C) Saving for long-term

WHAT STYLE OF BUDGET WOULD BE BEST FOR YOU?
A) Strict style—I want no room for error and would prefer to know where every single dollar spent goes.
B) Medium effort—I want to account for every dollar I spend without the hassle of tracking every transaction.
C) Minimal effort—I hate the idea of budgeting, but I want something that will help me achieve my financial goals.

WOULD YOU PREFER A MANUAL OR AUTOMATIC BUDGETING STYLE?
A) Manual
B) Mix of both
C) Automatic

MOSTLY A'S	A cash-based budget or basic spreadsheet might be a good option for you. With a cash-based budget, also known as an envelope-style budget, you will split your income up into envelopes each month. Label each envelope with a spending category that contains the exact amount of money that you plan to spend inside. Once you use that money up, you cannot allocate any additional income toward that expense. If you prefer to do this digitally, as you typically pay your bills online and find a digital method more convenient, you could follow suit by setting up a different bank account for each spending category. A spreadsheet can make any changes and tracking extremely simple by showing you exactly where your money is allocated.
MOSTLY B'S	Try zero-based budgeting or an app that can track your monthly spending habits. Zero-based budgets are a more hands-on way to organize your finances. In this style of budgeting, when you subtract your expenses from your income, you must always end at $0. Please note that expenses also include any money saved. This helps you account for every dollar spent and earned.

MOSTLY C'S	You may like the option of paying yourself first. Creating a budget can be a tedious process, especially for those of us who find it challenging to abide by the rules of a spreadsheet. If this sounds like you, it might be best to take on a style of budgeting that involves paying yourself first. Rather than focus on what goes where, prioritize automatic contributions to a separate account for your savings every payday. The rest of your income is free for variable expenses.
YOUR BUDGETING STYLE	

DAY 1

CONNECT & REFLECT

Current mood (circle one): ☺ ☺ ☹ 😣 😄 😴

I FEEL _____

_____

_____

MONEY IS CURRENTLY _____

_____

_____

I WANT MONEY TO _____

_____

_____

WHAT WERE CHALLENGES THAT I FACED TODAY?

1. _____

_____

2. _____

_____

3. _____

_____

WHAT ARE SUCCESSES THAT I ENJOYED TODAY?

1. _____

_____

2. _____

_____

3. _____

WHERE DO I STAND?

☐ I need to get back on track to achieve my financial goal.

☐ I am on track with my financial goal.

TODAY'S EXPENSES

BUDGET CATEGORY	ITEM	COST
TOTAL		

TODAY'S INCOME

ITEM	AMOUNT
TOTAL	

DAY 2

Date _____

CONNECT & REFLECT

Current mood (circle one): 🙂 😐 😖 😣 😆 😴

I FEEL _____

_____

_____

MONEY IS CURRENTLY _____

_____

_____

I WANT MONEY TO _____

_____

_____

WHAT WERE CHALLENGES THAT I FACED TODAY?

1. _____

_____

2. _____

_____

3. _____

_____

WHAT ARE SUCCESSES THAT I ENJOYED TODAY?

1. _____

_____

2. _____

_____

3. _____

WHERE DO I STAND?

☐ I need to get back on track to achieve my financial goal.

☐ I am on track with my financial goal.

TODAY'S EXPENSES

BUDGET CATEGORY	ITEM	COST
TOTAL		

TODAY'S INCOME

ITEM	AMOUNT
TOTAL	

DAY 3

Date _____

CONNECT & REFLECT

Current mood (circle one): ☺ ☺ ☹ 😫 😊 😴ᶻ

I FEEL _____

_____

_____

MONEY IS CURRENTLY _____

_____

_____

I WANT MONEY TO _____

_____

_____

WHAT WERE CHALLENGES THAT I FACED TODAY?

1. _____

_____

2. _____

_____

3. _____

_____

WHAT ARE SUCCESSES THAT I ENJOYED TODAY?

1. _____

_____

2. _____

_____

3. _____

☐ I need to get back on track to achieve my financial goal.

☐ I am on track with my financial goal.

TODAY'S EXPENSES

BUDGET CATEGORY	ITEM	COST
TOTAL		

TODAY'S INCOME

ITEM	AMOUNT
TOTAL	

DAY 4

CONNECT & REFLECT

Current mood (circle one): 😊 😐 😖 😆 😌 😴

I FEEL _____

_____

_____

MONEY IS CURRENTLY _____

_____

_____

I WANT MONEY TO _____

_____

_____

WHAT WERE CHALLENGES THAT I FACED TODAY?

1. _____

_____

2. _____

_____

3. _____

_____

WHAT ARE SUCCESSES THAT I ENJOYED TODAY?

1. _____

_____

2. _____

_____

3. _____

☐ I need to get back on track to achieve my financial goal.

☐ I am on track with my financial goal.

TODAY'S EXPENSES

BUDGET CATEGORY	ITEM	COST
TOTAL		

TODAY'S INCOME

ITEM	AMOUNT
TOTAL	

DAY 5

CONNECT & REFLECT

Current mood (circle one): ☺ ☺ ☹ 😖 😄 😴

I FEEL _____

_____

_____

MONEY IS CURRENTLY _____

_____

_____

I WANT MONEY TO _____

_____

_____

WHAT WERE CHALLENGES THAT I FACED TODAY?

1. _____

_____

2. _____

_____

3. _____

_____

WHAT ARE SUCCESSES THAT I ENJOYED TODAY?

1. _____

_____

2. _____

_____

3. _____

☐ I need to get back on track to achieve my financial goal.

☐ I am on track with my financial goal.

TODAY'S EXPENSES

BUDGET CATEGORY	ITEM	COST
TOTAL		

TODAY'S INCOME

ITEM	AMOUNT
TOTAL	

DAY 6

CONNECT & REFLECT

Current mood (circle one): ☺ ☺ ☹ 😆 😄 😴

I FEEL _____

_____

_____

MONEY IS CURRENTLY _____

_____

_____

I WANT MONEY TO _____

_____

_____

WHAT WERE CHALLENGES THAT I FACED TODAY?

1. _____

_____

2. _____

_____

3. _____

_____

WHAT ARE SUCCESSES THAT I ENJOYED TODAY?

1. _____

_____

2. _____

_____

3. _____

☐ I need to get back on track to achieve my financial goal.

☐ I am on track with my financial goal.

TODAY'S EXPENSES

BUDGET CATEGORY	ITEM	COST
TOTAL		

TODAY'S INCOME

ITEM	AMOUNT
TOTAL	

DAY 7

Date _____

CONNECT & REFLECT

Current mood (circle one): ☺ ☺ ☹ 😣 😄 😴

I FEEL _____
_____
_____

MONEY IS CURRENTLY _____
_____
_____

I WANT MONEY TO _____
_____
_____

WHAT WERE CHALLENGES THAT I FACED TODAY?

1. _____
_____

2. _____
_____

3. _____
_____

WHAT ARE SUCCESSES THAT I ENJOYED TODAY?

1. _____
_____

2. _____
_____

3. _____

☐ I need to get back on track to achieve my financial goal.

☐ I am on track with my financial goal.

TODAY'S EXPENSES

BUDGET CATEGORY	ITEM	COST
TOTAL		

TODAY'S INCOME

ITEM	AMOUNT
TOTAL	

WEEKLY OUTLOOK

What could you improve on financially this week?

_____

_____

_____

_____

_____

_____

What was the best financial decision you made last week?

_____

_____

_____

_____

_____

Next week's motivations:

1. _____

_____

_____

_____

2. _____

_____

_____

_____

3. _____

_____

_____

_____

I WILL _____

_____

_____

_____

I WILL NOT _____

_____

_____

I AM _____

_____

_____

LAST PURCHASE: _____

_____

COST: _____

_____

THIS WEEK'S SAVINGS: _____

TOTAL MONEY SAVED/DEBT REPAID SO FAR: _____

_____

CURRENT WANT(S): _____

_____

CURRENT NEED(S): _____

_____

THIS WEEK'S FOCUS: AUTOMATE & STREAMLINE

THE WHAT

The best part about living in a technologically advanced age is that we no longer have to remember everything. Your phone, watch, computer, and tablet are there to remind you: "Hey, silly, don't forget you have that thing today!" Banking and finance have come along for the ride, too. The world of Fintech, the digital technology that we use for our online financial services, is rapidly evolving. This means that your digital and automated options for saving and spending are becoming endless. You can also have your money work for you by using cashback credit cards, rewards apps, and memberships with retailers or coupon clubs.

THE WHY

One of the best ways to manage your finances is to set up automatic payments and contributions. It can make paying bills, receiving payments, and sending money to your savings accounts a breeze. All you need to do is ensure that you always have enough money in your bank account and let the Internet and apps do their thing. With rewards programs and cashback credit cards, you can use the points you earn to save money. From there, you can put those savings toward something else—like your financial goal!

THE HOW

For banking, there are many online options for opening high-interest savings accounts and setting up weekly or monthly contributions. For credit card companies and other organizations, setting up automatic payments is a great option. If you choose a credit card as your automatic payment option, just remember to pay it off in full each month if you can, to avoid interest.

BILL	DUE DATE	MONTHLY COST (ESTIMATE)	PAYMENT METHOD	SET UP AUTOMATIC PAYMENTS?

SAVINGS GOAL	MONTHLY CONTRI-BUTION	SAVINGS ACCOUNT	CONTRI-BUTION METHOD	SET UP AUTOMATIC CONTRI-BUTIONS?

DAY 8

CONNECT & REFLECT

Current mood (circle one): ☺ 😐 ☹ 😫 😆 😴ᶻ

I FEEL _____

_____

_____

MONEY IS CURRENTLY _____

_____

_____

I WANT MONEY TO _____

_____

_____

WHAT WERE CHALLENGES THAT I FACED TODAY?

1. _____

_____

2. _____

_____

3. _____

_____

WHAT ARE SUCCESSES THAT I ENJOYED TODAY?

1. _____

_____

2. _____

_____

3. _____

☐ I need to get back on track to achieve my financial goal.

☐ I am on track with my financial goal.

TODAY'S EXPENSES

BUDGET CATEGORY	ITEM	COST
TOTAL		

TODAY'S INCOME

ITEM	AMOUNT
TOTAL	

DAY 9

Date _____

CONNECT & REFLECT

Current mood (circle one): ☺ 😐 ☹ 😫 😄 😴

I FEEL _____

_____

_____

MONEY IS CURRENTLY _____

_____

_____

I WANT MONEY TO _____

_____

_____

WHAT WERE CHALLENGES THAT I FACED TODAY?

1. _____

_____

2. _____

_____

3. _____

_____

WHAT ARE SUCCESSES THAT I ENJOYED TODAY?

1. _____

_____

2. _____

_____

3. _____

☐ I need to get back on track to achieve my financial goal.

☐ I am on track with my financial goal.

TODAY'S EXPENSES

BUDGET CATEGORY	ITEM	COST
TOTAL		

TODAY'S INCOME

ITEM	AMOUNT
TOTAL	

DAY 10

Date _____

CONNECT & REFLECT

Current mood (circle one): ☺ ☻ ☹ 😣 😄 😴

I FEEL _____

_____

_____

MONEY IS CURRENTLY _____

_____

_____

I WANT MONEY TO _____

_____

_____

WHAT WERE CHALLENGES THAT I FACED TODAY?

1. _____

_____

2. _____

_____

3. _____

_____

WHAT ARE SUCCESSES THAT I ENJOYED TODAY?

1. _____

_____

2. _____

_____

3. _____

☐ I need to get back on track to achieve my financial goal.

☐ I am on track with my financial goal.

TODAY'S EXPENSES

BUDGET CATEGORY	ITEM	COST
TOTAL		

TODAY'S INCOME

ITEM	AMOUNT
TOTAL	

DAY 11

Date _____

CONNECT & REFLECT

Current mood (circle one): ☺ 😐 ☹ 😫 😄 😴

I FEEL _____

_____

_____

MONEY IS CURRENTLY _____

_____

_____

I WANT MONEY TO _____

_____

_____

WHAT WERE CHALLENGES THAT I FACED TODAY?

1. _____

_____

2. _____

_____

3. _____

_____

WHAT ARE SUCCESSES THAT I ENJOYED TODAY?

1. _____

_____

2. _____

_____

3. _____

☐ I need to get back on track to achieve my financial goal.

☐ I am on track with my financial goal.

TODAY'S EXPENSES

BUDGET CATEGORY	ITEM	COST
TOTAL		

TODAY'S INCOME

ITEM	AMOUNT
TOTAL	

DAY 12

CONNECT & REFLECT

Current mood (circle one): ☺ 😐 ☹ 😣 😄 😴ᶻ

I FEEL _____

_____

_____

MONEY IS CURRENTLY _____

_____

_____

I WANT MONEY TO _____

_____

_____

WHAT WERE CHALLENGES THAT I FACED TODAY?

1. _____

_____

2. _____

_____

3. _____

_____

WHAT ARE SUCCESSES THAT I ENJOYED TODAY?

1. _____

_____

2. _____

_____

3. _____

☐ I need to get back on track to achieve my financial goal.

☐ I am on track with my financial goal.

TODAY'S EXPENSES

BUDGET CATEGORY	ITEM	COST
TOTAL		

TODAY'S INCOME

ITEM	AMOUNT
TOTAL	

DAY 13

CONNECT & REFLECT

Current mood (circle one): 😊 😐 😣 😫 😆 😴

I FEEL _____

_____

_____

MONEY IS CURRENTLY _____

_____

_____

I WANT MONEY TO _____

_____

_____

WHAT WERE CHALLENGES THAT I FACED TODAY?

1. _____

_____

2. _____

_____

3. _____

_____

WHAT ARE SUCCESSES THAT I ENJOYED TODAY?

1. _____

_____

2. _____

_____

3. _____

☐ I need to get back on track to achieve my financial goal.

☐ I am on track with my financial goal.

TODAY'S EXPENSES

BUDGET CATEGORY	ITEM	COST
TOTAL		

TODAY'S INCOME

ITEM	AMOUNT
TOTAL	

DAY 14

CONNECT & REFLECT

Current mood (circle one): 🙂 😐 ☹️ 😫 😌 😴

I FEEL _____

_____

_____

MONEY IS CURRENTLY _____

_____

_____

I WANT MONEY TO _____

_____

_____

WHAT WERE CHALLENGES THAT I FACED TODAY?

1. _____

_____

2. _____

_____

3. _____

_____

WHAT ARE SUCCESSES THAT I ENJOYED TODAY?

1. _____

_____

2. _____

_____

3. _____

WHERE DO I STAND?

☐ I need to get back on track to achieve my financial goal.

☐ I am on track with my financial goal.

TODAY'S EXPENSES

BUDGET CATEGORY	ITEM	COST
TOTAL		

TODAY'S INCOME

ITEM	AMOUNT
TOTAL	

WEEKLY OUTLOOK

What could you improve on financially this week?

_____

_____

_____

_____

_____

_____

What was the best financial decision you made last week?

_____

_____

_____

_____

_____

Next week's motivations:

1. _____

_____

_____

_____

2. _____

_____

_____

_____

3. _____

_____

_____

_____

I WILL _____

_____

_____

_____

I WILL NOT _____

_____

_____

I AM _____

_____

_____

LAST PURCHASE: _____

_____

COST: _____

_____

THIS WEEK'S SAVINGS: _____

TOTAL MONEY SAVED/DEBT REPAID SO FAR: _____

_____

CURRENT WANT(S): _____

_____

CURRENT NEED(S): _____

_____

THIS WEEK'S FOCUS: CONTROL YOUR HABITS

THE WHAT

To accomplish any financial goal, you need to ensure that your money habits are only going to help you achieve success. Whether you want to focus on controlling your impulse purchases or cutting back on your discretionary spending, now is a good time to learn to balance these changes and control your spending habits.

THE WHY

Every purchase that you don't need to make is a trip that takes away money that you could have put toward your day-to-day expenses or your financial goal. That being said, life isn't fun when you don't allow yourself to enjoy your money so it's important to find a balanced approach to curb your impulse purchases.

THE HOW

Find a strategy that helps you to control your spending. You can also plan for the money that you don't think you'll spend. If you set aside a part of your budget for annual discretionary expenses, you won't need to worry when making these types of purchases.

What are purchases I tend to buy impulsively?

1. _____
2. _____
3. _____

When am I most likely to buy impulsively?

1. _____
2. _____
3. _____

Choose your most common impulse purchase:

_____

Look back at your expenses for the past six months. How much did you spend on that item?

Weekly average: $_____

Monthly average: $_____

The estimated annual total for this expense (multiply your monthly average by 12): $_____

Can you decrease the amount you spend each month?

☐ Yes   ☐ No

If yes, choose a lower amount:

_____

If no, stick with the current average. Work these expenses into your budget.

DAY 15

CONNECT & REFLECT

Current mood (circle one): ☺ 😐 ☹ 😬 😆 😴ᶻ

I FEEL _____

_____

_____

MONEY IS CURRENTLY _____

_____

_____

I WANT MONEY TO _____

_____

_____

WHAT WERE CHALLENGES THAT I FACED TODAY?

1. _____

_____

2. _____

_____

3. _____

_____

WHAT ARE SUCCESSES THAT I ENJOYED TODAY?

1. _____

_____

2. _____

_____

3. _____

☐ I need to get back on track to achieve my financial goal.

☐ I am on track with my financial goal.

TODAY'S EXPENSES

BUDGET CATEGORY	ITEM	COST
TOTAL		

TODAY'S INCOME

ITEM	AMOUNT
TOTAL	

DAY 16

Date _____

CONNECT & REFLECT

Current mood (circle one): ☺ 😐 ☹ 😣 😆 😴ᶻ

I FEEL _____

_____

_____

MONEY IS CURRENTLY _____

_____

_____

I WANT MONEY TO _____

_____

_____

WHAT WERE CHALLENGES THAT I FACED TODAY?

1. _____

_____

2. _____

_____

3. _____

_____

WHAT ARE SUCCESSES THAT I ENJOYED TODAY?

1. _____

_____

2. _____

_____

3. _____

WHERE DO I STAND?

☐ I need to get back on track to achieve my financial goal.

☐ I am on track with my financial goal.

TODAY'S EXPENSES

BUDGET CATEGORY	ITEM	COST
TOTAL		

TODAY'S INCOME

ITEM	AMOUNT
TOTAL	

DAY 17

CONNECT & REFLECT

Current mood (circle one): ☺ ☺ ☹ 😫 😊 😴ᶻ

I FEEL _____

_____

_____

MONEY IS CURRENTLY _____

_____

_____

I WANT MONEY TO _____

_____

_____

WHAT WERE CHALLENGES THAT I FACED TODAY?

1. _____

_____

2. _____

_____

3. _____

_____

WHAT ARE SUCCESSES THAT I ENJOYED TODAY?

1. _____

_____

2. _____

_____

3. _____

WHERE DO I STAND?

☐ I need to get back on track to achieve my financial goal.

☐ I am on track with my financial goal.

TODAY'S EXPENSES

BUDGET CATEGORY	ITEM	COST
TOTAL		

TODAY'S INCOME

ITEM	AMOUNT
TOTAL	

DAY 18

CONNECT & REFLECT

Current mood (circle one): ☺ 😐 ☹ 😣 😄 😴ᶻ

I FEEL _____

_____

_____

MONEY IS CURRENTLY _____

_____

_____

I WANT MONEY TO _____

_____

_____

WHAT WERE CHALLENGES THAT I FACED TODAY?

1. _____

_____

2. _____

_____

3. _____

_____

WHAT ARE SUCCESSES THAT I ENJOYED TODAY?

1. _____

_____

2. _____

_____

3. _____

☐ I need to get back on track to achieve my financial goal.

☐ I am on track with my financial goal.

TODAY'S EXPENSES

BUDGET CATEGORY	ITEM	COST
TOTAL		

TODAY'S INCOME

ITEM	AMOUNT
TOTAL	

DAY 19

CONNECT & REFLECT

Current mood (circle one): 😊 😐 😣 😆 😌 😴

I FEEL _____

_____

_____

MONEY IS CURRENTLY _____

_____

_____

I WANT MONEY TO _____

_____

_____

WHAT WERE CHALLENGES THAT I FACED TODAY?

1. _____

_____

2. _____

_____

3. _____

_____

WHAT ARE SUCCESSES THAT I ENJOYED TODAY?

1. _____

_____

2. _____

_____

3. _____

☐ I need to get back on track to achieve my financial goal.

☐ I am on track with my financial goal.

TODAY'S EXPENSES

BUDGET CATEGORY	ITEM	COST
TOTAL		

TODAY'S INCOME

ITEM	AMOUNT
TOTAL	

DAY 20

CONNECT & REFLECT

Current mood (circle one): ☺ 😐 ☹ 😖 😄 😴ᶻ

I FEEL _____

_____

_____

MONEY IS CURRENTLY _____

_____

_____

I WANT MONEY TO _____

_____

_____

WHAT WERE CHALLENGES THAT I FACED TODAY?

1. _____

_____

2. _____

_____

3. _____

_____

WHAT ARE SUCCESSES THAT I ENJOYED TODAY?

1. _____

_____

2. _____

_____

3. _____

□ I need to get back on track to achieve my financial goal.

□ I am on track with my financial goal.

TODAY'S EXPENSES

BUDGET CATEGORY	ITEM	COST
TOTAL		

TODAY'S INCOME

ITEM	AMOUNT
TOTAL	

DAY 21

Date _____

CONNECT & REFLECT

Current mood (circle one): ☺ 😐 ☹ 😫 😄 😴ᶻ

I FEEL _____

_____

_____

MONEY IS CURRENTLY _____

_____

_____

I WANT MONEY TO _____

_____

_____

WHAT WERE CHALLENGES THAT I FACED TODAY?

1. _____

_____

2. _____

_____

3. _____

_____

WHAT ARE SUCCESSES THAT I ENJOYED TODAY?

1. _____

_____

2. _____

_____

3. _____

☐ I need to get back on track to achieve my financial goal.

☐ I am on track with my financial goal.

TODAY'S EXPENSES

BUDGET CATEGORY	ITEM	COST
TOTAL		

TODAY'S INCOME

ITEM	AMOUNT
TOTAL	

WEEKLY OUTLOOK

What could you improve on financially this week?

_____

_____

_____

_____

_____

_____

What was the best financial decision you made last week?

_____

_____

_____

_____

_____

Next week's motivations:

1. _____

_____

_____

_____

2. _____

_____

_____

_____

3. _____

_____

_____

_____

I WILL _____

_____

_____

_____

I WILL NOT _____

_____

_____

I AM _____

_____

_____

LAST PURCHASE: _____

_____

COST: _____

_____

THIS WEEK'S SAVINGS: _____

TOTAL MONEY SAVED/DEBT REPAID SO FAR: _____

_____

CURRENT WANT(S): _____

_____

CURRENT NEED(S): _____

_____

THIS WEEK'S FOCUS: EDUCATE & GROW

THE WHAT

We've all been known to make mistakes with our money here and there. Some of us are impulsive, meaning we'll do something reckless without consideration for its consequences. Others are just tired and completely missed that no-parking zone sign that resulted in an expensive ticket.

I'm asking you to not let your past mistakes or your lack of knowledge about money to stop you from tackling your financial situation. So what if you're "bad" at money? So what if you make mistakes every once in awhile? Now is the time to learn and grow along the way.

THE WHY

As with anything in life, the more time you take to educate yourself in something, the more of an expert you become. Personal finance is no different. If you don't challenge yourself, you miss out on opportunities to grow. Don't be discouraged if one tactic or strategy from this journal does not work for you. Nothing, except working toward a goal, is for everyone.

THE HOW

Search for different resources that encourage your desire to learn about money. Your journey with your finances is one of the best places to look. Reflecting on past financial mistakes or current challenges can tell you what you need to do to move forward. Remind yourself about what motivates you to be better with your money. Push yourself out of your comfort zone. There is no end to what you can change and learn when it comes to money.

What financial challenges are you facing on your current journey?

1. _____

2. _____

3. _____

What lessons have you learned about your finances so far?

1. _____

2. _____

3. _____

What are some of your biggest financial mistakes or regrets?

1. _____

2. _____

3. _____

What did you learn from these mistakes?

1. _____

2. _____

3. _____

DAY 22

CONNECT & REFLECT

Current mood (circle one): ☺ 😐 ☹ 😆 😄 😴

I FEEL _____

_____

_____

MONEY IS CURRENTLY _____

_____

_____

I WANT MONEY TO _____

_____

_____

WHAT WERE CHALLENGES THAT I FACED TODAY?

1. _____

_____

2. _____

_____

3. _____

_____

WHAT ARE SUCCESSES THAT I ENJOYED TODAY?

1. _____

_____

2. _____

_____

3. _____

☐ I need to get back on track to achieve my financial goal.

☐ I am on track with my financial goal.

TODAY'S EXPENSES

BUDGET CATEGORY	ITEM	COST
TOTAL		

TODAY'S INCOME

ITEM	AMOUNT
TOTAL	

DAY 23

Date _____

CONNECT & REFLECT

Current mood (circle one): ☺ ☺ ☹ 😫 😄 😴ᶻ

I FEEL _____

_____

_____

MONEY IS CURRENTLY _____

_____

_____

I WANT MONEY TO _____

_____

_____

WHAT WERE CHALLENGES THAT I FACED TODAY?

1. _____

_____

2. _____

_____

3. _____

_____

WHAT ARE SUCCESSES THAT I ENJOYED TODAY?

1. _____

_____

2. _____

_____

3. _____

☐ I need to get back on track to achieve my financial goal.

☐ I am on track with my financial goal.

TODAY'S EXPENSES

BUDGET CATEGORY	ITEM	COST
TOTAL		

TODAY'S INCOME

ITEM	AMOUNT
TOTAL	

DAY 24

CONNECT & REFLECT

Current mood (circle one): 😊 😐 😣 😫 😄 😴

I FEEL _____

_____

_____

MONEY IS CURRENTLY _____

_____

_____

I WANT MONEY TO _____

_____

_____

WHAT WERE CHALLENGES THAT I FACED TODAY?

1. _____

_____

2. _____

_____

3. _____

_____

WHAT ARE SUCCESSES THAT I ENJOYED TODAY?

1. _____

_____

2. _____

_____

3. _____

☐ I need to get back on track to achieve my financial goal.

☐ I am on track with my financial goal.

TODAY'S EXPENSES

BUDGET CATEGORY	ITEM	COST
TOTAL		

TODAY'S INCOME

ITEM	AMOUNT
TOTAL	

DAY 25

Date _____

CONNECT & REFLECT

Current mood (circle one): ☺ ☺ ☹ 😣 😄 😴ᶻᶻ

I FEEL _____

_____

_____

MONEY IS CURRENTLY _____

_____

_____

I WANT MONEY TO _____

_____

_____

WHAT WERE CHALLENGES THAT I FACED TODAY?

1. _____

_____

2. _____

_____

3. _____

_____

WHAT ARE SUCCESSES THAT I ENJOYED TODAY?

1. _____

_____

2. _____

_____

3. _____

☐ I need to get back on track to achieve my financial goal.

☐ I am on track with my financial goal.

TODAY'S EXPENSES

BUDGET CATEGORY	ITEM	COST
TOTAL		

TODAY'S INCOME

ITEM	AMOUNT
TOTAL	

DAY 26

CONNECT & REFLECT

Current mood (circle one): ☺ 😐 ☹ 😫 😄 😴

I FEEL _____

_____

_____

MONEY IS CURRENTLY _____

_____

_____

I WANT MONEY TO _____

_____

_____

WHAT WERE CHALLENGES THAT I FACED TODAY?

1. _____

_____

2. _____

_____

3. _____

_____

WHAT ARE SUCCESSES THAT I ENJOYED TODAY?

1. _____

_____

2. _____

_____

3. _____

☐ I need to get back on track to achieve my financial goal.

☐ I am on track with my financial goal.

TODAY'S EXPENSES

BUDGET CATEGORY	ITEM	COST
TOTAL		

TODAY'S INCOME

ITEM	AMOUNT
TOTAL	

DAY 27

Date _____

CONNECT & REFLECT

Current mood (circle one): ☺ 😐 😣 😖 😄 😴ᶻ

I FEEL _____

_____

_____

MONEY IS CURRENTLY _____

_____

_____

I WANT MONEY TO _____

_____

_____

WHAT WERE CHALLENGES THAT I FACED TODAY?

1. _____

_____

2. _____

_____

3. _____

_____

WHAT ARE SUCCESSES THAT I ENJOYED TODAY?

1. _____

_____

2. _____

_____

3. _____

☐ I need to get back on track to achieve my financial goal.

☐ I am on track with my financial goal.

TODAY'S EXPENSES

BUDGET CATEGORY	ITEM	COST
TOTAL		

TODAY'S INCOME

ITEM	AMOUNT
TOTAL	

DAY 28

CONNECT & REFLECT

Current mood (circle one): ☺ ☺ ☹ 😣 😄 😴ᶻ

I FEEL _____

_____

_____

MONEY IS CURRENTLY _____

_____

_____

I WANT MONEY TO _____

_____

_____

WHAT WERE CHALLENGES THAT I FACED TODAY?

1. _____

_____

2. _____

_____

3. _____

_____

WHAT ARE SUCCESSES THAT I ENJOYED TODAY?

1. _____

_____

2. _____

_____

3. _____

☐ I need to get back on track to achieve my financial goal.

☐ I am on track with my financial goal.

TODAY'S EXPENSES

BUDGET CATEGORY	ITEM	COST
TOTAL		

TODAY'S INCOME

ITEM	AMOUNT
TOTAL	

WEEKLY OUTLOOK

What could you improve on financially this week?

_____

_____

_____

_____

_____

_____

What was the best financial decision you made last week?

_____

_____

_____

_____

_____

Next week's motivations:

1. _____

_____

_____

_____

2. _____

_____

_____

_____

3. _____

_____

_____

_____

I WILL _____

_____

_____

_____

I WILL NOT _____

_____

_____

I AM _____

_____

_____

LAST PURCHASE: _____

_____

COST: _____

_____

THIS WEEK'S SAVINGS: _____

TOTAL MONEY SAVED/DEBT REPAID SO FAR: _____

_____

CURRENT WANT(S): _____

_____

CURRENT NEED(S): _____

_____

THIS WEEK'S FOCUS: HOLD YOURSELF ACCOUNTABLE

THE WHAT

Anyone who has money knows that they will occasionally slip up, even if they are the most organized person in the world. We have a budget, we've automated our money, and we've taken a good look at our spending habits, but that doesn't mean you don't need to stay on top of your finances. The number-one enemy of any financial goal is complacency. The moment you become too comfortable is the moment you lose your motivation and desire to succeed. There is no room for lethargy in your financial future. It's time to hold yourself accountable.

THE WHY

If you don't stay accountable, it can become effortless to start a free fall. You don't want to wind up in Never-Never-Planned, the city that spends money it doesn't have. It's essential to hold yourself accountable by doing monthly check-ins to monitor any unplanned or surprise purchases that you might have made. This way, you remind yourself that you have to stick to your budget as often as possible to stay on track with your goal. If you don't review your goals and plans every single day, who else is going to do that for you? Embrace your finances by staying on top of your tasks.

THE HOW

Writing in your journal every single day is fantastic, but sometimes it takes even more than that. Let's look back at your spending over the past three weeks starting with Day 1 (page 24). From there, write down anything that stands out as an unplanned or unexpected expense, and note if you went over your budget in any spending category. Ask yourself if these expenses were a one-time thing, or if it's time to change where you allocate your money each month.

UNEXPECTED EXPENSES

DATE	BUDGET CATEGORY	ITEM	COST	WAS THIS A ONE-TIME PURCHASE?	WAS THIS OVER BUDGET?

DAY 29

Date _____

CONNECT & REFLECT

Current mood (circle one): ☺ 😐 ☹ 😣 😄 😴ᶻ

I FEEL _____

_____

_____

MONEY IS CURRENTLY _____

_____

_____

I WANT MONEY TO _____

_____

_____

WHAT WERE CHALLENGES THAT I FACED TODAY?

1. _____

_____

2. _____

_____

3. _____

_____

WHAT ARE SUCCESSES THAT I ENJOYED TODAY?

1. _____

_____

2. _____

_____

3. _____

☐ I need to get back on track to achieve my financial goal.

☐ I am on track with my financial goal.

TODAY'S EXPENSES

BUDGET CATEGORY	ITEM	COST
TOTAL		

TODAY'S INCOME

ITEM	AMOUNT
TOTAL	

DAY 30

Date _____

CONNECT & REFLECT

Current mood (circle one): ☺ 😐 ☹ 😬 😄 😴

I FEEL _____

_____

_____

MONEY IS CURRENTLY _____

_____

_____

I WANT MONEY TO _____

_____

_____

WHAT WERE CHALLENGES THAT I FACED TODAY?

1. _____

_____

2. _____

_____

3. _____

_____

WHAT ARE SUCCESSES THAT I ENJOYED TODAY?

1. _____

_____

2. _____

_____

3. _____

☐ I need to get back on track to achieve my financial goal.

☐ I am on track with my financial goal.

TODAY'S EXPENSES

BUDGET CATEGORY	ITEM	COST
TOTAL		

TODAY'S INCOME

ITEM	AMOUNT
TOTAL	

DAY 31

CONNECT & REFLECT

Current mood (circle one): ☺ ☹ ☹ 😫 😄 😴

I FEEL _____

_____

_____

MONEY IS CURRENTLY _____

_____

_____

I WANT MONEY TO _____

_____

_____

WHAT WERE CHALLENGES THAT I FACED TODAY?

1. _____

_____

2. _____

_____

3. _____

_____

WHAT ARE SUCCESSES THAT I ENJOYED TODAY?

1. _____

_____

2. _____

_____

3. _____

☐ I need to get back on track to achieve my financial goal.

☐ I am on track with my financial goal.

TODAY'S EXPENSES

BUDGET CATEGORY	ITEM	COST
TOTAL		

TODAY'S INCOME

ITEM	AMOUNT
TOTAL	

Date _____

CONNECT & REFLECT

Current mood (circle one): ☺ 😐 🙁 😫 😄 😴ᶻ

I FEEL _____

_____

_____

MONEY IS CURRENTLY _____

_____

_____

I WANT MONEY TO _____

_____

_____

WHAT WERE CHALLENGES THAT I FACED TODAY?

1. _____

_____

2. _____

_____

3. _____

_____

WHAT ARE SUCCESSES THAT I ENJOYED TODAY?

1. _____

_____

2. _____

_____

3. _____

☐ I need to get back on track to achieve my financial goal.

☐ I am on track with my financial goal.

TODAY'S EXPENSES

BUDGET CATEGORY	ITEM	COST
TOTAL		

TODAY'S INCOME

ITEM	AMOUNT
TOTAL	

DAY 33

CONNECT & REFLECT

Current mood (circle one): 😊 😐 😣 😆 😂 😴

I FEEL _____

_____

_____

MONEY IS CURRENTLY _____

_____

_____

I WANT MONEY TO _____

_____

_____

WHAT WERE CHALLENGES THAT I FACED TODAY?

1. _____

_____

2. _____

_____

3. _____

_____

WHAT ARE SUCCESSES THAT I ENJOYED TODAY?

1. _____

_____

2. _____

_____

3. _____

WHERE DO I STAND?

☐ I need to get back on track to achieve my financial goal.

☐ I am on track with my financial goal.

TODAY'S EXPENSES

BUDGET CATEGORY	ITEM	COST
TOTAL		

TODAY'S INCOME

ITEM	AMOUNT
TOTAL	

DAY 34

CONNECT & REFLECT

Current mood (circle one): ☺ 😐 ☹ 😫 😄 😴ᶻ

I FEEL _____

_____

_____

MONEY IS CURRENTLY _____

_____

_____

I WANT MONEY TO _____

_____

_____

WHAT WERE CHALLENGES THAT I FACED TODAY?

1. _____

_____

2. _____

_____

3. _____

_____

WHAT ARE SUCCESSES THAT I ENJOYED TODAY?

1. _____

_____

2. _____

_____

3. _____

WHERE DO I STAND?

☐ I need to get back on track to achieve my financial goal.

☐ I am on track with my financial goal.

TODAY'S EXPENSES

BUDGET CATEGORY	ITEM	COST
TOTAL		

TODAY'S INCOME

ITEM	AMOUNT
TOTAL	

DAY 35

CONNECT & REFLECT

Current mood (circle one): ☺ 😐 ☹ 😫 😆 😴

I FEEL _____

_____

_____

MONEY IS CURRENTLY _____

_____

_____

I WANT MONEY TO _____

_____

_____

WHAT WERE CHALLENGES THAT I FACED TODAY?

1. _____

_____

2. _____

_____

3. _____

_____

WHAT ARE SUCCESSES THAT I ENJOYED TODAY?

1. _____

_____

2. _____

_____

3. _____

☐ I need to get back on track to achieve my financial goal.

☐ I am on track with my financial goal.

TODAY'S EXPENSES

BUDGET CATEGORY	ITEM	COST
TOTAL		

TODAY'S INCOME

ITEM	AMOUNT
TOTAL	

WEEKLY OUTLOOK

What could you improve on financially this week?

_____
_____
_____
_____
_____
_____

What was the best financial decision you made last week?

_____
_____
_____
_____
_____

Next week's motivations:

1. _____
_____
_____
_____

2. _____
_____
_____
_____

3. _____
_____
_____
_____

I WILL _____

_____

_____

_____

I WILL NOT _____

_____

_____

I AM _____

_____

_____

LAST PURCHASE: _____

_____

COST: _____

_____

THIS WEEK'S SAVINGS: _____

TOTAL MONEY SAVED/DEBT REPAID SO FAR: _____

_____

CURRENT WANT(S): _____

_____

CURRENT NEED(S): _____

_____

THIS WEEK'S FOCUS: UNDERSTAND YOUR SURROUNDINGS

THE WHAT

Have you ever heard that quote by Jim Rohn that you are the average of the five people you spend the most time with? He's not wrong. Picture your five closest friends or family members right now and compare how they live their lives to yours. We are creatures of habit, and the factors that influence how we spend our time and money aren't always a mystery. Take some time to get to know how your family and friends save—and you might realize you manage your finances similarly.

THE WHY

The people closest to us may have some of the best and creative ideas about money. Do they have any lessons that would be worthwhile to write down? It can not only broaden your perspective but also introduce the topic of money in a way that is flattering rather than nosy.

THE HOW

Ask some people you trust some money questions. Sometimes the best lessons are lessons learned from loved ones.

THE INTERVIEW

Name: _____

Relation: _____

Occupation: _____

1. How does your loved one manage their finances?

_____

_____

_____

2. What are some ways this person saves money?

_____

_____

_____

3. What is the best piece of financial advice they have ever received?

_____

_____

_____

4. What was their income at their very first job?

_____

_____

_____

5. What did they pay for their very first vehicle?

_____

_____

_____

6. What did they pay for their very first mortgage or rent?

_____

_____

_____

DAY 36

Date _____

CONNECT & REFLECT

Current mood (circle one): ☺ 😐 ☹ 😬 😆 😴ᶻ

I FEEL _____

_____

_____

MONEY IS CURRENTLY _____

_____

_____

I WANT MONEY TO _____

_____

_____

WHAT WERE CHALLENGES THAT I FACED TODAY?

1. _____

_____

2. _____

_____

3. _____

_____

WHAT ARE SUCCESSES THAT I ENJOYED TODAY?

1. _____

_____

2. _____

_____

3. _____

☐ I need to get back on track to achieve my financial goal.

☐ I am on track with my financial goal.

TODAY'S EXPENSES

BUDGET CATEGORY	ITEM	COST
TOTAL		

TODAY'S INCOME

ITEM	AMOUNT
TOTAL	

DAY 37

Date _____

CONNECT & REFLECT

Current mood (circle one): 😊 😐 ☹️ 😖 😄 😴

I FEEL _____

_____

_____

MONEY IS CURRENTLY _____

_____

_____

I WANT MONEY TO _____

_____

_____

WHAT WERE CHALLENGES THAT I FACED TODAY?

1. _____

_____

2. _____

_____

3. _____

_____

WHAT ARE SUCCESSES THAT I ENJOYED TODAY?

1. _____

_____

2. _____

_____

3. _____

☐ I need to get back on track to achieve my financial goal.

☐ I am on track with my financial goal.

TODAY'S EXPENSES

BUDGET CATEGORY	ITEM	COST
TOTAL		

TODAY'S INCOME

ITEM	AMOUNT
TOTAL	

DAY 38

CONNECT & REFLECT

Current mood (circle one): 😊 😐 😦 😣 😄 😴ᶻ

I FEEL _____

_____

_____

MONEY IS CURRENTLY _____

_____

_____

I WANT MONEY TO _____

_____

_____

WHAT WERE CHALLENGES THAT I FACED TODAY?

1. _____

_____

2. _____

_____

3. _____

_____

WHAT ARE SUCCESSES THAT I ENJOYED TODAY?

1. _____

_____

2. _____

_____

3. _____

☐ I need to get back on track to achieve my financial goal.

☐ I am on track with my financial goal.

TODAY'S EXPENSES

BUDGET CATEGORY	ITEM	COST
TOTAL		

TODAY'S INCOME

ITEM	AMOUNT
TOTAL	

DAY 39

CONNECT & REFLECT

Current mood (circle one): ☺ 😐 ☹ 😆 😄 😴

I FEEL _____

_____

_____

MONEY IS CURRENTLY _____

_____

_____

I WANT MONEY TO _____

_____

_____

WHAT WERE CHALLENGES THAT I FACED TODAY?

1. _____

_____

2. _____

_____

3. _____

_____

WHAT ARE SUCCESSES THAT I ENJOYED TODAY?

1. _____

_____

2. _____

_____

3. _____

☐ I need to get back on track to achieve my financial goal.

☐ I am on track with my financial goal.

TODAY'S EXPENSES

BUDGET CATEGORY	ITEM	COST
TOTAL		

TODAY'S INCOME

ITEM	AMOUNT
TOTAL	

DAY 40

CONNECT & REFLECT

Current mood (circle one): ☺ ☺ ☹ 😫 😄 😴ᶻ

I FEEL _____

_____

_____

MONEY IS CURRENTLY _____

_____

_____

I WANT MONEY TO _____

_____

_____

WHAT WERE CHALLENGES THAT I FACED TODAY?

1. _____

_____

2. _____

_____

3. _____

_____

WHAT ARE SUCCESSES THAT I ENJOYED TODAY?

1. _____

_____

2. _____

_____

3. _____

☐ I need to get back on track to achieve my financial goal.

☐ I am on track with my financial goal.

TODAY'S EXPENSES

BUDGET CATEGORY	ITEM	COST
TOTAL		

TODAY'S INCOME

ITEM	AMOUNT
TOTAL	

DAY 41

Date _____

CONNECT & REFLECT

Current mood (circle one): 🙂 😐 ☹️ 😬 😆 😴

I FEEL _____

_____

_____

MONEY IS CURRENTLY _____

_____

_____

I WANT MONEY TO _____

_____

_____

WHAT WERE CHALLENGES THAT I FACED TODAY?

1. _____

_____

2. _____

_____

3. _____

_____

WHAT ARE SUCCESSES THAT I ENJOYED TODAY?

1. _____

_____

2. _____

_____

3. _____

☐ I need to get back on track to achieve my financial goal.

☐ I am on track with my financial goal.

TODAY'S EXPENSES

BUDGET CATEGORY	ITEM	COST
TOTAL		

TODAY'S INCOME

ITEM	AMOUNT
TOTAL	

DAY 42

CONNECT & REFLECT

Current mood (circle one): ☺ ☻ ☹ 😫 😌 😴

I FEEL _____

_____

_____

MONEY IS CURRENTLY _____

_____

_____

I WANT MONEY TO _____

_____

_____

WHAT WERE CHALLENGES THAT I FACED TODAY?

1. _____

_____

2. _____

_____

3. _____

_____

WHAT ARE SUCCESSES THAT I ENJOYED TODAY?

1. _____

_____

2. _____

_____

3. _____

☐ I need to get back on track to achieve my financial goal.

☐ I am on track with my financial goal.

TODAY'S EXPENSES

BUDGET CATEGORY	ITEM	COST
TOTAL		

TODAY'S INCOME

ITEM	AMOUNT
TOTAL	

WEEKLY OUTLOOK

What could you improve on financially this week?

_____

_____

_____

_____

_____

_____

What was the best financial decision you made last week?

_____

_____

_____

_____

_____

Next week's motivations:

1. _____

_____

_____

_____

2. _____

_____

_____

_____

3. _____

_____

_____

_____

I WILL _____

_____

_____

_____

I WILL NOT _____

_____

_____

I AM _____

_____

_____

LAST PURCHASE: _____

_____

COST: _____

_____

THIS WEEK'S SAVINGS: _____

TOTAL MONEY SAVED/DEBT REPAID SO FAR: _____

_____

CURRENT WANT(S): _____

_____

CURRENT NEED(S): _____

_____

THIS WEEK'S FOCUS: HALFWAY CHECK-IN

THE WHAT

Now that we're halfway to our financial goal, you may find yourself settling into a routine. Now is an excellent time to be honest with yourself and your money to see where you are. It's also a great time to check in on your mental health, especially since money often plays a significant role in how people feel about themselves and their achievements in life.

THE WHY

A check-in ensures that you are on the right track and can make any necessary corrections to your budget or goal. Mental health check-ins will ensure that you aren't overwhelmed and that you are happy with your progress, both in your financial situation and your personal life. It might seem silly to have to remind yourself to check in on how you feel, but sometimes it's necessary. Well, all the time, really.

THE HOW

Let's look at your current savings, how much more you have to save, and whether you need to save more per day, per week, per month, or however you're tracking it. If you are doing well and have no worries about your financial goal, don't feel like you need to review your goal. Instead, find some ways to give yourself a break from all this goal-setting and enjoy your success. Planning some money-free activities can be useful, whether you are doing well or struggling to keep to your financial goal. Although setting a lofty goal is intense, it's a good idea to focus on the lighter parts of your experience.

Current money saved/debt repaid	
Financial goal	

You are _____ days away from your financial goal.

You need to save $_____/day to achieve your financial goal on time.

Are you on track to finish your goal?   ☐ Yes   ☐ No

If no, try to adjust some of your financial habits in the few weeks to come. Perhaps you can attempt a "no-spend weekend" in which you plan to stay in and put any money you would have originally spent (in going out) toward your financial goal.

Are there any habits or behaviors that are holding you back from achieving your goal?

1. _____

2. _____

3. _____

What are some activities or ways you could address these habits or behaviors?

1. _____

2. _____

3. _____

Make a plan to accomplish these activities:

_____
_____
_____

DAY 43

CONNECT & REFLECT

Current mood (circle one): ☺ ☻ ☹ 😆 😂 😴

I FEEL _____

_____

_____

MONEY IS CURRENTLY _____

_____

_____

I WANT MONEY TO _____

_____

_____

WHAT WERE CHALLENGES THAT I FACED TODAY?

1. _____

_____

2. _____

_____

3. _____

_____

WHAT ARE SUCCESSES THAT I ENJOYED TODAY?

1. _____

_____

2. _____

_____

3. _____

☐ I need to get back on track to achieve my financial goal.

☐ I am on track with my financial goal.

TODAY'S EXPENSES

BUDGET CATEGORY	ITEM	COST
TOTAL		

TODAY'S INCOME

ITEM	AMOUNT
TOTAL	

DAY 44

CONNECT & REFLECT

Current mood (circle one): 😊 😐 ☹️ 😫 😆 😴ᶻ

I FEEL _____

_____

_____

MONEY IS CURRENTLY _____

_____

_____

I WANT MONEY TO _____

_____

_____

WHAT WERE CHALLENGES THAT I FACED TODAY?

1. _____

_____

2. _____

_____

3. _____

_____

WHAT ARE SUCCESSES THAT I ENJOYED TODAY?

1. _____

_____

2. _____

_____

3. _____

☐ I need to get back on track to achieve my financial goal.

☐ I am on track with my financial goal.

TODAY'S EXPENSES

BUDGET CATEGORY	ITEM	COST
TOTAL		

TODAY'S INCOME

ITEM	AMOUNT
TOTAL	

DAY 45

CONNECT & REFLECT

Current mood (circle one): ☺ ☺ ☹ 😖 😄 😴

I FEEL _____

_____

_____

MONEY IS CURRENTLY _____

_____

_____

I WANT MONEY TO _____

_____

_____

WHAT WERE CHALLENGES THAT I FACED TODAY?

1. _____

_____

2. _____

_____

3. _____

_____

WHAT ARE SUCCESSES THAT I ENJOYED TODAY?

1. _____

_____

2. _____

_____

3. _____

☐ I need to get back on track to achieve my financial goal.

☐ I am on track with my financial goal.

TODAY'S EXPENSES

BUDGET CATEGORY	ITEM	COST
TOTAL		

TODAY'S INCOME

ITEM	AMOUNT
TOTAL	

DAY 46

CONNECT & REFLECT

Current mood (circle one): ☺ 😐 ☹ 😫 😄 😴

I FEEL _____

_____

_____

MONEY IS CURRENTLY _____

_____

_____

I WANT MONEY TO _____

_____

_____

WHAT WERE CHALLENGES THAT I FACED TODAY?

1. _____

_____

2. _____

_____

3. _____

_____

WHAT ARE SUCCESSES THAT I ENJOYED TODAY?

1. _____

_____

2. _____

_____

3. _____

☐ I need to get back on track to achieve my financial goal.

☐ I am on track with my financial goal.

TODAY'S EXPENSES

BUDGET CATEGORY	ITEM	COST
TOTAL		

TODAY'S INCOME

ITEM	AMOUNT
TOTAL	

DAY 47

CONNECT & REFLECT

Current mood (circle one): ☺ 😐 ☹ 😖 😄 😴

I FEEL _____

_____

_____

MONEY IS CURRENTLY _____

_____

_____

I WANT MONEY TO _____

_____

_____

WHAT WERE CHALLENGES THAT I FACED TODAY?

1. _____

_____

2. _____

_____

3. _____

_____

WHAT ARE SUCCESSES THAT I ENJOYED TODAY?

1. _____

_____

2. _____

_____

3. _____

☐ I need to get back on track to achieve my financial goal.

☐ I am on track with my financial goal.

TODAY'S EXPENSES

BUDGET CATEGORY	ITEM	COST
TOTAL		

TODAY'S INCOME

ITEM	AMOUNT
TOTAL	

DAY 48

Date _____

CONNECT & REFLECT

Current mood (circle one): ☺ 😐 ☹ 😆 😂 😴

I FEEL _____

_____

_____

MONEY IS CURRENTLY _____

_____

_____

I WANT MONEY TO _____

_____

_____

WHAT WERE CHALLENGES THAT I FACED TODAY?

1. _____

_____

2. _____

_____

3. _____

_____

WHAT ARE SUCCESSES THAT I ENJOYED TODAY?

1. _____

_____

2. _____

_____

3. _____

☐ I need to get back on track to achieve my financial goal.

☐ I am on track with my financial goal.

TODAY'S EXPENSES

BUDGET CATEGORY	ITEM	COST
TOTAL		

TODAY'S INCOME

ITEM	AMOUNT
TOTAL	

DAY 49

CONNECT & REFLECT

Current mood (circle one): ☺ 😐 ☹ 😖 😄 😴

I FEEL _____

_____

_____

MONEY IS CURRENTLY _____

_____

_____

I WANT MONEY TO _____

_____

_____

WHAT WERE CHALLENGES THAT I FACED TODAY?

1. _____

_____

2. _____

_____

3. _____

_____

WHAT ARE SUCCESSES THAT I ENJOYED TODAY?

1. _____

_____

2. _____

_____

3. _____

☐ I need to get back on track to achieve my financial goal.

☐ I am on track with my financial goal.

TODAY'S EXPENSES

BUDGET CATEGORY	ITEM	COST
TOTAL		

TODAY'S INCOME

ITEM	AMOUNT
TOTAL	

WEEKLY OUTLOOK

What could you improve on financially this week?

_____

_____

_____

_____

_____

_____

What was the best financial decision you made last week?

_____

_____

_____

_____

_____

Next week's motivations:

1. _____

_____

_____

_____

2. _____

_____

_____

_____

3. _____

_____

_____

_____

I WILL _____

_____

_____

_____

I WILL NOT _____

_____

_____

I AM _____

_____

_____

LAST PURCHASE: _____

_____

COST: _____

_____

THIS WEEK'S SAVINGS: _____

TOTAL MONEY SAVED/DEBT REPAID SO FAR: _____

_____

CURRENT WANT(S): _____

_____

CURRENT NEED(S): _____

_____

THIS WEEK'S FOCUS: BE FINANCIALLY SECURE

THE WHAT

These days, everything in our lives is online. Picture of your dog? Online. The presentation you made in school? Online. Video of your last trip to Europe? Online. As we saw in Week 2, there is no escaping the digital world—especially when it comes to your finances. Therefore, it's even more important to protect them.

One fundamental way to protect your digital assets (and money saved in any bank account) is to ensure that you have proper protection from fraudulent activity. Although banks are the most common storage unit for cash, it is still imperative that you keep an eye on your accounts. It's easy to avoid looking at your bank accounts if you're embarrassed about your savings or debt, but the danger with this habit is that you might miss potential signs of suspicious activity.

THE WHY

No one will ever care more about your money than you. Scammers and hackers are more common than ever, making it necessary to stay on top of your earnings and livelihood. It would be tough to see $1,000 go missing from your checking account without your realizing it, and then needing to dip into overdraft to cover your rent. Don't let this happen to you. Being proactive ensures that the information stored on your accounts is private and inaccessible to others as well.

THE HOW

It's a good idea to ensure you are up to date in every sense of the word when it comes to your digital financial life. It's time to change your passwords (and make sure you don't use the same one for every account), check your banking statements, set up alerts, and get some new security questions. You can also learn about the protection your bank offers from fraudulent activity and get in the habit of monitoring your accounts as often as possible. The more regularly you do it, the more you'll understand your own money, and in turn, notice when things aren't right. Let's go through this ultimate task list.

TASK COMPLETED?	Y / N
Update your passwords (smartphone included).	
Check your credit score and report.	
Use a different password for each financial tool.	
Back up your data.	
Get life insurance.	
Get home insurance.	
Update vehicle insurance.	
Create a will.	
Create an estate plan for your social media accounts.	
Keep an external hard drive to back up any legal documents, such as a will or estate plan.	
Ensure all of your financial apps have proper encryption.	
Use secure websites (e.g., URLs that begin with "https").	
Remove stored credit card numbers from all online shopping sites.	
Set a regular reminder to review banking for suspicious activity.	
Install that software update you've been ignoring.	

DAY 50

CONNECT & REFLECT

Current mood (circle one): ☺ 😐 ☹ 😣 😄 😴

I FEEL _____

_____

_____

MONEY IS CURRENTLY _____

_____

_____

I WANT MONEY TO _____

_____

_____

WHAT WERE CHALLENGES THAT I FACED TODAY?

1. _____

_____

2. _____

_____

3. _____

_____

WHAT ARE SUCCESSES THAT I ENJOYED TODAY?

1. _____

_____

2. _____

_____

3. _____

☐ I need to get back on track to achieve my financial goal.

☐ I am on track with my financial goal.

TODAY'S EXPENSES

BUDGET CATEGORY	ITEM	COST
TOTAL		

TODAY'S INCOME

ITEM	AMOUNT
TOTAL	

DAY 51

CONNECT & REFLECT

Current mood (circle one): ☺ 😐 ☹ 😣 😄 😴

I FEEL _____

_____

_____

MONEY IS CURRENTLY _____

_____

_____

I WANT MONEY TO _____

_____

_____

WHAT WERE CHALLENGES THAT I FACED TODAY?

1. _____

_____

2. _____

_____

3. _____

_____

WHAT ARE SUCCESSES THAT I ENJOYED TODAY?

1. _____

_____

2. _____

_____

3. _____

☐ I need to get back on track to achieve my financial goal.

☐ I am on track with my financial goal.

TODAY'S EXPENSES

BUDGET CATEGORY	ITEM	COST
TOTAL		

TODAY'S INCOME

ITEM	AMOUNT
TOTAL	

DAY 52

Date _____

CONNECT & REFLECT

Current mood (circle one): 🙂 😐 🙁 😫 😄 😴

I FEEL _____

_____

_____

MONEY IS CURRENTLY _____

_____

_____

I WANT MONEY TO _____

_____

_____

WHAT WERE CHALLENGES THAT I FACED TODAY?

1. _____

_____

2. _____

_____

3. _____

_____

WHAT ARE SUCCESSES THAT I ENJOYED TODAY?

1. _____

_____

2. _____

_____

3. _____

☐ I need to get back on track to achieve my financial goal.

☐ I am on track with my financial goal.

TODAY'S EXPENSES

BUDGET CATEGORY	ITEM	COST
TOTAL		

TODAY'S INCOME

ITEM	AMOUNT
TOTAL	

DAY 53

CONNECT & REFLECT

Current mood (circle one): ☺ 😐 ☹ 😫 😂 😴

I FEEL _____

_____

_____

MONEY IS CURRENTLY _____

_____

_____

I WANT MONEY TO _____

_____

_____

WHAT WERE CHALLENGES THAT I FACED TODAY?

1. _____

_____

2. _____

_____

3. _____

_____

WHAT ARE SUCCESSES THAT I ENJOYED TODAY?

1. _____

_____

2. _____

_____

3. _____

☐ I need to get back on track to achieve my financial goal.

☐ I am on track with my financial goal.

TODAY'S EXPENSES

BUDGET CATEGORY	ITEM	COST
TOTAL		

TODAY'S INCOME

ITEM	AMOUNT
TOTAL	

DAY 54

Date _____

CONNECT & REFLECT

Current mood (circle one): ☺ 😐 ☹ 😫 😄 😴ᶻᶻ

I FEEL _____

_____

_____

MONEY IS CURRENTLY _____

_____

_____

I WANT MONEY TO _____

_____

_____

WHAT WERE CHALLENGES THAT I FACED TODAY?

1. _____

_____

2. _____

_____

3. _____

_____

WHAT ARE SUCCESSES THAT I ENJOYED TODAY?

1. _____

_____

2. _____

_____

3. _____

☐ I need to get back on track to achieve my financial goal.

☐ I am on track with my financial goal.

TODAY'S EXPENSES

BUDGET CATEGORY	ITEM	COST
TOTAL		

TODAY'S INCOME

ITEM	AMOUNT
TOTAL	

DAY 55

CONNECT & REFLECT

Current mood (circle one): ☺ 😐 ☹ 😆 😄 😴

I FEEL _____

_____

_____

MONEY IS CURRENTLY _____

_____

_____

I WANT MONEY TO _____

_____

_____

WHAT WERE CHALLENGES THAT I FACED TODAY?

1. _____

_____

2. _____

_____

3. _____

_____

WHAT ARE SUCCESSES THAT I ENJOYED TODAY?

1. _____

_____

2. _____

_____

3. _____

☐ I need to get back on track to achieve my financial goal.

☐ I am on track with my financial goal.

TODAY'S EXPENSES

BUDGET CATEGORY	ITEM	COST
TOTAL		

TODAY'S INCOME

ITEM	AMOUNT
TOTAL	

DAY 56

CONNECT & REFLECT

Current mood (circle one): ☺ ☺ ☹ 😣 😄 😴ᶻᶻ

I FEEL _____

_____

_____

MONEY IS CURRENTLY _____

_____

_____

I WANT MONEY TO _____

_____

_____

WHAT WERE CHALLENGES THAT I FACED TODAY?

1. _____

_____

2. _____

_____

3. _____

_____

WHAT ARE SUCCESSES THAT I ENJOYED TODAY?

1. _____

_____

2. _____

_____

3. _____

☐ I need to get back on track to achieve my financial goal.

☐ I am on track with my financial goal.

TODAY'S EXPENSES

BUDGET CATEGORY	ITEM	COST
TOTAL		

TODAY'S INCOME

ITEM	AMOUNT
TOTAL	

WEEKLY OUTLOOK

What could you improve on financially this week?

_____

_____

_____

_____

_____

_____

What was the best financial decision you made last week?

_____

_____

_____

_____

_____

Next week's motivations:

1. _____

_____

_____

_____

2. _____

_____

_____

_____

3. _____

_____

_____

_____

I WILL _____

_____

_____

_____

I WILL NOT _____

_____

_____

I AM _____

_____

_____

LAST PURCHASE: _____

_____

COST: _____

_____

THIS WEEK'S SAVINGS: _____

TOTAL MONEY SAVED/DEBT REPAID SO FAR: _____

_____

CURRENT WANT(S): _____

_____

CURRENT NEED(S): _____

_____

THIS WEEK'S FOCUS: LEARN TO BALANCE

THE WHAT

Since you've started working on your goal, you've probably felt much more restricted with your spending than you have in the past. After all, to achieve any goal, you're often required to put a ton of energy and effort into that game plan and nothing else. Saving money or paying off debt is no different, but it's important to remember that money is also something to be enjoyed. For example, you can justify expenses that are related to your passions and hobbies. If you love to work out or play video games, you can find a way to afford these activities.

THE WHY

Money doesn't have to be all frugal and no fun. We've set our treat-yourself rewards for when we hit a more substantial milestone, but what about in your everyday life? Are you supposed to turn down every fun event or every coffee date that comes your way? Of course not. But you do need to find a time and a place. Hobbies not only make us happier, but also help us meet like-minded people, earn a side income, or relieve stress after a tough week at work.

THE HOW

It's time to get to know what makes you happy after you spend. Then, be sure to work your passions into your budget, if necessary. You know that you will spend money on these parts of your life, regardless of whether or not you have money saved to do so. Be financially savvy enough to stay ahead of your hobbies. What purchases always make you happy?

1. _____

2. _____

3. _____

4. _____

5. _____

6. _____

Do you need to set a limit on discretionary purchases?
☐ Yes   ☐ No

If you've answered yes, what is the limit?

_____

Before you make these purchases, ask yourself the following:

☐ Are my basic financial needs covered?

☐ Will this purchase put me over budget or in debt?

☐ Do I have an emergency fund to cover surprise expenses?

☐ Am I saving for retirement?

☐ If I make this purchase, will it provide me with a great memory or experience?

If you still feel confident in a purchase after considering the above factors, you likely need or want this item or experience. Therefore, don't restrict yourself from enjoying your hard-earned money.

DAY 57

CONNECT & REFLECT

Current mood (circle one): ☺ 😐 ☹ 😖 😄 😴

I FEEL _____

_____

_____

MONEY IS CURRENTLY _____

_____

_____

I WANT MONEY TO _____

_____

_____

WHAT WERE CHALLENGES THAT I FACED TODAY?

1. _____

_____

2. _____

_____

3. _____

_____

WHAT ARE SUCCESSES THAT I ENJOYED TODAY?

1. _____

_____

2. _____

_____

3. _____

WHERE DO I STAND?

☐ I need to get back on track to achieve my financial goal.

☐ I am on track with my financial goal.

TODAY'S EXPENSES

BUDGET CATEGORY	ITEM	COST
TOTAL		

TODAY'S INCOME

ITEM	AMOUNT
TOTAL	

DAY 58

CONNECT & REFLECT

Current mood (circle one): ☺ 😐 ☹ 😬 😆 😴ᶻ

I FEEL _____

_____

_____

MONEY IS CURRENTLY _____

_____

_____

I WANT MONEY TO _____

_____

_____

WHAT WERE CHALLENGES THAT I FACED TODAY?

1. _____

_____

2. _____

_____

3. _____

_____

WHAT ARE SUCCESSES THAT I ENJOYED TODAY?

1. _____

_____

2. _____

_____

3. _____

☐ I need to get back on track to achieve my financial goal.

☐ I am on track with my financial goal.

TODAY'S EXPENSES

BUDGET CATEGORY	ITEM	COST
TOTAL		

TODAY'S INCOME

ITEM	AMOUNT
TOTAL	

DAY 59

CONNECT & REFLECT

Current mood (circle one): ☺ 😐 ☹ 😫 😌 😴ᶻᶻ

I FEEL _____

_____

_____

MONEY IS CURRENTLY _____

_____

_____

I WANT MONEY TO _____

_____

_____

WHAT WERE CHALLENGES THAT I FACED TODAY?

1. _____

_____

2. _____

_____

3. _____

_____

WHAT ARE SUCCESSES THAT I ENJOYED TODAY?

1. _____

_____

2. _____

_____

3. _____

☐ I need to get back on track to achieve my financial goal.

☐ I am on track with my financial goal.

TODAY'S EXPENSES

BUDGET CATEGORY	ITEM	COST
TOTAL		

TODAY'S INCOME

ITEM	AMOUNT
TOTAL	

DAY 60

CONNECT & REFLECT

Current mood (circle one): ☺ 😐 ☹ 😫 😆 😴

I FEEL _____

_____

_____

MONEY IS CURRENTLY _____

_____

_____

I WANT MONEY TO _____

_____

_____

WHAT WERE CHALLENGES THAT I FACED TODAY?

1. _____

_____

2. _____

_____

3. _____

_____

WHAT ARE SUCCESSES THAT I ENJOYED TODAY?

1. _____

_____

2. _____

_____

3. _____

☐ I need to get back on track to achieve my financial goal.

☐ I am on track with my financial goal.

TODAY'S EXPENSES

BUDGET CATEGORY	ITEM	COST
TOTAL		

TODAY'S INCOME

ITEM	AMOUNT
TOTAL	

DAY 61

Date _____

CONNECT & REFLECT

Current mood (circle one): ☺ 😐 😧 😖 😆 😴

I FEEL _____

_____

_____

MONEY IS CURRENTLY _____

_____

_____

I WANT MONEY TO _____

_____

_____

WHAT WERE CHALLENGES THAT I FACED TODAY?

1. _____

_____

2. _____

_____

3. _____

_____

WHAT ARE SUCCESSES THAT I ENJOYED TODAY?

1. _____

_____

2. _____

_____

3. _____

☐ I need to get back on track to achieve my financial goal.

☐ I am on track with my financial goal.

TODAY'S EXPENSES

BUDGET CATEGORY	ITEM	COST
TOTAL		

TODAY'S INCOME

ITEM	AMOUNT
TOTAL	

DAY 62

CONNECT & REFLECT

Current mood (circle one): ☺ 😐 ☹ 😫 😋 😴

I FEEL _____

_____

_____

MONEY IS CURRENTLY _____

_____

_____

I WANT MONEY TO _____

_____

_____

WHAT WERE CHALLENGES THAT I FACED TODAY?

1. _____

_____

2. _____

_____

3. _____

_____

WHAT ARE SUCCESSES THAT I ENJOYED TODAY?

1. _____

_____

2. _____

_____

3. _____

☐ I need to get back on track to achieve my financial goal.

☐ I am on track with my financial goal.

TODAY'S EXPENSES

BUDGET CATEGORY	ITEM	COST
TOTAL		

TODAY'S INCOME

ITEM	AMOUNT
TOTAL	

DAY 63

Date _____

CONNECT & REFLECT

Current mood (circle one): ☺ 😐 ☹ 😫 😄 😴ᶻ

I FEEL _____

_____

_____

MONEY IS CURRENTLY _____

_____

_____

I WANT MONEY TO _____

_____

_____

WHAT WERE CHALLENGES THAT I FACED TODAY?

1. _____

_____

2. _____

_____

3. _____

_____

WHAT ARE SUCCESSES THAT I ENJOYED TODAY?

1. _____

_____

2. _____

_____

3. _____

WHERE DO I STAND?

☐ I need to get back on track to achieve my financial goal.

☐ I am on track with my financial goal.

TODAY'S EXPENSES

BUDGET CATEGORY	ITEM	COST
TOTAL		

TODAY'S INCOME

ITEM	AMOUNT
TOTAL	

WEEKLY OUTLOOK

What could you improve on financially this week?

_____

_____

_____

_____

_____

_____

What was the best financial decision you made last week?

_____

_____

_____

_____

_____

Next week's motivations:

1. _____

_____

_____

_____

2. _____

_____

_____

_____

3. _____

_____

_____

_____

I WILL _____

_____

_____

_____

I WILL NOT _____

_____

_____

I AM _____

_____

_____

LAST PURCHASE: _____

_____

COST: _____

_____

THIS WEEK'S SAVINGS: _____

TOTAL MONEY SAVED/DEBT REPAID SO FAR: _____

_____

CURRENT WANT(S): _____

_____

CURRENT NEED(S): _____

_____

THIS WEEK'S FOCUS: TIPS & TRICKS TOOLBOX

THE WHAT

It's time to make your financial toolbelt even stronger than it already is by introducing some great ways to make financial decisions and manage your spending habits. Financial tricks can come in handy any time you are planning to make a purchase.

The first trick is the "cost-per-use" trick. If you feel as though you need to buy a new item, estimate the number of times you will use that item, divide the cost by that number, and think about whether that would be a reasonable cost. If you are considering a new pair of jeans for $300, and you estimate you will wear those jeans around 20 times, that means that your jeans will cost you $15 each time you wear them.

The second trick is to control your spending by making your life less convenient. The harder it is to spend, the less likely you'll do it. Maybe it's time to disable contactless payments on your cards, log out of your digital payment apps, set spending limits on your credit cards, and only take cash to places where you tend to overspend. Let's bring back the days when you forget your wallet at home, and you don't have the option to spend money.

I like to call the last trick the "put-it-back-jack" rule. Every time that you are shopping, you must put one item back or remove one thing from your cart before you check out. This way, you can avoid any extra add-ons or any purchases that you might not actually need.

THE WHY

When you see how much you spend each day on nonessentials, you put things into perspective pretty quickly. If you want to ensure that you are making a worthwhile purchase, take some time and do the math. It's not always as hard as it seems.

THE HOW

To take advantage of all of these tips and tricks in one shot, let's look at a previous shopping trip you've made. Review each item's "cost-per-use," review how you paid for these items, and choose one of the items from your receipt that you could have put back before checking out.

Find one of your most recent receipts. What was your original budget for this shopping trip? $ _____

What were some of the items you could have done without?

1. _____

2. _____

3. _____

4. _____

5. _____

6. _____

Total cost of these items: $ _____

Did these additional items put you over budget?   ☐ Yes   ☐ No

What would you have put back now that you are home, and why?

1. _____

2. _____

3. _____

DAY 64

CONNECT & REFLECT

Current mood (circle one):   ☺ 😐 ☹ 😬 😄 😴

I FEEL _____

_____

_____

MONEY IS CURRENTLY _____

_____

_____

I WANT MONEY TO _____

_____

_____

WHAT WERE CHALLENGES THAT I FACED TODAY?

1. _____

_____

2. _____

_____

3. _____

_____

WHAT ARE SUCCESSES THAT I ENJOYED TODAY?

1. _____

_____

2. _____

_____

3. _____

☐ I need to get back on track to achieve my financial goal.

☐ I am on track with my financial goal.

TODAY'S EXPENSES

BUDGET CATEGORY	ITEM	COST
TOTAL		

TODAY'S INCOME

ITEM	AMOUNT
TOTAL	

DAY 65

Date _____

CONNECT & REFLECT

Current mood (circle one): ☺ 😐 ☹ 😫 😄 😴ᶻ

I FEEL _____

_____

_____

MONEY IS CURRENTLY _____

_____

_____

I WANT MONEY TO _____

_____

_____

WHAT WERE CHALLENGES THAT I FACED TODAY?

1. _____

_____

2. _____

_____

3. _____

_____

WHAT ARE SUCCESSES THAT I ENJOYED TODAY?

1. _____

_____

2. _____

_____

3. _____

☐ I need to get back on track to achieve my financial goal.

☐ I am on track with my financial goal.

TODAY'S EXPENSES

BUDGET CATEGORY	ITEM	COST
TOTAL		

TODAY'S INCOME

ITEM	AMOUNT
TOTAL	

DAY 66

CONNECT & REFLECT

Current mood (circle one): ☺ 😐 ☹ 😫 😄 😴ᶻ

I FEEL _____

_____

_____

MONEY IS CURRENTLY _____

_____

_____

I WANT MONEY TO _____

_____

_____

WHAT WERE CHALLENGES THAT I FACED TODAY?

1. _____

_____

2. _____

_____

3. _____

_____

WHAT ARE SUCCESSES THAT I ENJOYED TODAY?

1. _____

_____

2. _____

_____

3. _____

☐ I need to get back on track to achieve my financial goal.

☐ I am on track with my financial goal.

TODAY'S EXPENSES

BUDGET CATEGORY	ITEM	COST
TOTAL		

TODAY'S INCOME

ITEM	AMOUNT
TOTAL	

DAY 67

Date _____

CONNECT & REFLECT

Current mood (circle one): ☺ ☺ ☹ 😆 😄 😴ᶻ

I FEEL _____

_____

_____

MONEY IS CURRENTLY _____

_____

_____

I WANT MONEY TO _____

_____

_____

WHAT WERE CHALLENGES THAT I FACED TODAY?

1. _____

_____

2. _____

_____

3. _____

_____

WHAT ARE SUCCESSES THAT I ENJOYED TODAY?

1. _____

_____

2. _____

_____

3. _____

☐ I need to get back on track to achieve my financial goal.

☐ I am on track with my financial goal.

TODAY'S EXPENSES

BUDGET CATEGORY	ITEM	COST
TOTAL		

TODAY'S INCOME

ITEM	AMOUNT
TOTAL	

DAY 68

Date _____

CONNECT & REFLECT

Current mood (circle one): ☺ 😐 ☹ 😣 😄 😴

I FEEL _____

_____

_____

MONEY IS CURRENTLY _____

_____

_____

I WANT MONEY TO _____

_____

_____

WHAT WERE CHALLENGES THAT I FACED TODAY?

1. _____

_____

2. _____

_____

3. _____

_____

WHAT ARE SUCCESSES THAT I ENJOYED TODAY?

1. _____

_____

2. _____

_____

3. _____

☐ I need to get back on track to achieve my financial goal.

☐ I am on track with my financial goal.

TODAY'S EXPENSES

BUDGET CATEGORY	ITEM	COST
TOTAL		

TODAY'S INCOME

ITEM	AMOUNT
TOTAL	

DAY 69

CONNECT & REFLECT

Current mood (circle one): ☺ ☻ ☹ 😣 😄 😴

I FEEL _____

_____

_____

MONEY IS CURRENTLY _____

_____

_____

I WANT MONEY TO _____

_____

_____

WHAT WERE CHALLENGES THAT I FACED TODAY?

1. _____

_____

2. _____

_____

3. _____

_____

WHAT ARE SUCCESSES THAT I ENJOYED TODAY?

1. _____

_____

2. _____

_____

3. _____

☐ I need to get back on track to achieve my financial goal.

☐ I am on track with my financial goal.

TODAY'S EXPENSES

BUDGET CATEGORY	ITEM	COST
TOTAL		

TODAY'S INCOME

ITEM	AMOUNT
TOTAL	

DAY 70

Date _____

CONNECT & REFLECT

Current mood (circle one): ☺ 😐 ☹ 😣 😆 😴ᶻ

I FEEL _____

_____

_____

MONEY IS CURRENTLY _____

_____

_____

I WANT MONEY TO _____

_____

_____

WHAT WERE CHALLENGES THAT I FACED TODAY?

1. _____

_____

2. _____

_____

3. _____

_____

WHAT ARE SUCCESSES THAT I ENJOYED TODAY?

1. _____

_____

2. _____

_____

3. _____

☐ I need to get back on track to achieve my financial goal.

☐ I am on track with my financial goal.

TODAY'S EXPENSES

BUDGET CATEGORY	ITEM	COST
TOTAL		

TODAY'S INCOME

ITEM	AMOUNT
TOTAL	

WEEKLY OUTLOOK

What could you improve on financially this week?

_____

_____

_____

_____

_____

_____

What was the best financial decision you made last week?

_____

_____

_____

_____

_____

Next week's motivations:

1. _____

_____

_____

_____

2. _____

_____

_____

_____

3. _____

_____

_____

_____

I WILL _____

_____

_____

_____

I WILL NOT _____

_____

_____

I AM _____

_____

_____

LAST PURCHASE: _____

_____

COST: _____

_____

THIS WEEK'S SAVINGS: _____

TOTAL MONEY SAVED/DEBT REPAID SO FAR: _____

_____

CURRENT WANT(S): _____

_____

CURRENT NEED(S): _____

_____

THIS WEEK'S FOCUS: INVEST IN THE FUTURE

THE WHAT

In the past eleven weeks, you've learned all about budgets, balance, and balancing budgets, as well as tools to control your financial behaviors. The one thing left to try is the one thing that most people find incredibly intimidating: investing. You might be wondering *Am I even ready to invest?* If you have paid off your debt, started to save, and have set financial goals, you likely are. If not, don't worry. Everything you are doing right now has put you on track to start soon.

Do you have a financial planner? Better yet, do you know what a financial planner does? Of course, they plan finances; but how? Typically, financial planners advise you on the best ways to save, invest, and spend your money. They help set you up with financial products and prepare you for retirement in a way that requires minimal effort, because they usually take on the hardship of organizing your financial life for you. Sounds pretty great, right?

If you want to keep your financial planning expenses minimal, robo-investing can come into play. One of the most popular ways to invest your money is through an online investing platform that manages your investments for you; you can link up to your bank accounts to automatically contribute into a robo-investment account each month. The best part? Some of these platforms require no minimum contribution.

THE WHY

For most people, their fears of investing lie in the assumptions that there is only one way to invest and that it requires a ton of money. They're not wrong, but the world of investing has come far. Companies have changed, and they are interested in your money—just as you should be. Investing can be difficult because it takes a certain risk tolerance, can come across as complex, and contains way too much financial jargon. Don't let those reasons scare you off. These days you don't have to be an expert to get started.

The most important part about choosing the company that manages your money is that you do your research. Always consider your long-term goals and whether you'd like to choose stocks yourself before you start making moves. Do a background check on the products that you choose to use, and find someone that has your best interests at heart when it comes to organizing your financial future.

THE HOW

Look at all your options. If you currently have money invested, are these the best places for you to invest? You need to understand how you'd like to invest and what types of investments are best for you.

If you are in the market for some help managing your money, try to find a fee-based planner over a commission-based planner. Fee-based planners will be up front with any costs associated with their services and have a fiduciary responsibility to put your needs as a shareholder first and foremost. In contrast, commission-based planners will often try to sell you products that make them a higher percentage of income. If you are interested in robo-investing, do some research into popular platforms to see if they are a good fit for you. How do you know which investing option is right for you? Let's find out.

OPTION 1: ROBO-INVESTING

1. Are you concerned about your financial future and in need of guidance?

   ☐ Yes ☐ No

2. Do you enjoy taking care of your own money?

   ☐ Yes ☐ No

3. Are you comfortable letting someone else control your finances?

   ☐ Yes ☐ No

4. Do you feel you would benefit from a third party to help make tough financial decisions?

   ☐ Yes ☐ No

5. Do you want to invest but are limited by the amount of money you can contribute?

   ☐ Yes ☐ No

6. Do you want to invest but are unsure where to start?

   ☐ Yes ☐ No

7. Do you prefer to manage all of your finances online or through apps?

   ☐ Yes ☐ No

8. Would you require a low-fee option to begin your journey into investing?

   ☐ Yes ☐ No

If you answered yes to more than three of the above questions, it might be a good idea to consider a robo-investing platform that you can trust to help manage your money.

OPTION 2: FINANCIAL PLANNER

1. Are you concerned about your financial future and in need of guidance?
   ☐ Yes ☐ No

2. Do you enjoy taking care of your own money?
   ☐ Yes ☐ No

3. Are you comfortable letting someone else control your finances?
   ☐ Yes ☐ No

4. Do you feel you would benefit from a third party to help make tough financial decisions?
   ☐ Yes ☐ No

5. Are you nearing retirement?
   ☐ Yes ☐ No

6. Have you recently started a family?
   ☐ Yes ☐ No

7. Are you self-employed?
   ☐ Yes ☐ No

8. Have you recently come into a lot of money, or do you currently have an above average net worth (think six figures)?
   ☐ Yes ☐ No

If you answered yes to more than three of the above questions, it might be a good idea to consider hiring a fee-based financial planner that you can trust to help manage your money.

Don't quite feel ready to invest yet? List the ways you are working toward this opportunity.

1. _____

2. _____

3. _____

DAY 71

Date _____

CONNECT & REFLECT

Current mood (circle one): ☺ 😐 ☹ 😖 😄 😴ᶻᶻ

I FEEL _____

_____

_____

MONEY IS CURRENTLY _____

_____

_____

I WANT MONEY TO _____

_____

_____

WHAT WERE CHALLENGES THAT I FACED TODAY?

1. _____

_____

2. _____

_____

3. _____

_____

WHAT ARE SUCCESSES THAT I ENJOYED TODAY?

1. _____

_____

2. _____

_____

3. _____

☐ I need to get back on track to achieve my financial goal.

☐ I am on track with my financial goal.

TODAY'S EXPENSES

BUDGET CATEGORY	ITEM	COST
TOTAL		

TODAY'S INCOME

ITEM	AMOUNT
TOTAL	

DAY 72

CONNECT & REFLECT

Current mood (circle one): ☺ 😐 ☹ 😫 😄 😴

I FEEL _____

_____

_____

MONEY IS CURRENTLY _____

_____

_____

I WANT MONEY TO _____

_____

_____

WHAT WERE CHALLENGES THAT I FACED TODAY?

1. _____

_____

2. _____

_____

3. _____

_____

WHAT ARE SUCCESSES THAT I ENJOYED TODAY?

1. _____

_____

2. _____

_____

3. _____

☐ I need to get back on track to achieve my financial goal.

☐ I am on track with my financial goal.

TODAY'S EXPENSES

BUDGET CATEGORY	ITEM	COST
TOTAL		

TODAY'S INCOME

ITEM	AMOUNT
TOTAL	

DAY 73

CONNECT & REFLECT

Current mood (circle one): 😊 😐 😖 😫 😆 😴

I FEEL _____

_____

_____

MONEY IS CURRENTLY _____

_____

_____

I WANT MONEY TO _____

_____

_____

WHAT WERE CHALLENGES THAT I FACED TODAY?

1. _____

_____

2. _____

_____

3. _____

_____

WHAT ARE SUCCESSES THAT I ENJOYED TODAY?

1. _____

_____

2. _____

_____

3. _____

☐ I need to get back on track to achieve my financial goal.

☐ I am on track with my financial goal.

TODAY'S EXPENSES

BUDGET CATEGORY	ITEM	COST
TOTAL		

TODAY'S INCOME

ITEM	AMOUNT
TOTAL	

DAY 74

Date _____

CONNECT & REFLECT

Current mood (circle one): ☺ 😐 ☹ 😆 😄 😴

I FEEL _____
_____
_____

MONEY IS CURRENTLY _____
_____
_____

I WANT MONEY TO _____
_____
_____

WHAT WERE CHALLENGES THAT I FACED TODAY?

1. _____
_____

2. _____
_____

3. _____
_____

WHAT ARE SUCCESSES THAT I ENJOYED TODAY?

1. _____
_____

2. _____
_____

3. _____

☐ I need to get back on track to achieve my financial goal.

☐ I am on track with my financial goal.

TODAY'S EXPENSES

BUDGET CATEGORY	ITEM	COST
TOTAL		

TODAY'S INCOME

ITEM	AMOUNT
TOTAL	

DAY 75

CONNECT & REFLECT

Current mood (circle one): ☺ 😐 ☹ 😫 😄 😴

I FEEL _____

_____

_____

MONEY IS CURRENTLY _____

_____

_____

I WANT MONEY TO _____

_____

_____

WHAT WERE CHALLENGES THAT I FACED TODAY?

1. _____

_____

2. _____

_____

3. _____

_____

WHAT ARE SUCCESSES THAT I ENJOYED TODAY?

1. _____

_____

2. _____

_____

3. _____

☐ I need to get back on track to achieve my financial goal.

☐ I am on track with my financial goal.

TODAY'S EXPENSES

BUDGET CATEGORY	ITEM	COST
TOTAL		

TODAY'S INCOME

ITEM	AMOUNT
TOTAL	

DAY 76

CONNECT & REFLECT

Current mood (circle one): ☺ 😐 ☹ 😆 😄 😴ᶻ

I FEEL _____

_____

_____

MONEY IS CURRENTLY _____

_____

_____

I WANT MONEY TO _____

_____

_____

WHAT WERE CHALLENGES THAT I FACED TODAY?

1. _____

_____

2. _____

_____

3. _____

_____

WHAT ARE SUCCESSES THAT I ENJOYED TODAY?

1. _____

_____

2. _____

_____

3. _____

☐ I need to get back on track to achieve my financial goal.

☐ I am on track with my financial goal.

TODAY'S EXPENSES

BUDGET CATEGORY	ITEM	COST
TOTAL		

TODAY'S INCOME

ITEM	AMOUNT
TOTAL	

DAY 77

CONNECT & REFLECT

Current mood (circle one): ☺ 😐 ☹ 😫 😄 😴ᶻ

I FEEL _____

_____

_____

MONEY IS CURRENTLY _____

_____

_____

I WANT MONEY TO _____

_____

_____

WHAT WERE CHALLENGES THAT I FACED TODAY?

1. _____

_____

2. _____

_____

3. _____

_____

WHAT ARE SUCCESSES THAT I ENJOYED TODAY?

1. _____

_____

2. _____

_____

3. _____

☐ I need to get back on track to achieve my financial goal.

☐ I am on track with my financial goal.

TODAY'S EXPENSES

BUDGET CATEGORY	ITEM	COST
TOTAL		

TODAY'S INCOME

ITEM	AMOUNT
TOTAL	

WEEKLY OUTLOOK

What could you improve on financially this week?

_____

_____

_____

_____

_____

_____

What was the best financial decision you made last week?

_____

_____

_____

_____

_____

Next week's motivations:

1. _____

_____

_____

_____

2. _____

_____

_____

_____

3. _____

_____

_____

_____

I WILL _____

_____

_____

_____

I WILL NOT _____

_____

_____

I AM _____

_____

_____

LAST PURCHASE: _____

_____

COST: _____

_____

THIS WEEK'S SAVINGS: _____

TOTAL MONEY SAVED/DEBT REPAID SO FAR: _____

_____

CURRENT WANT(S): _____

_____

CURRENT NEED(S): _____

_____

THIS WEEK'S FOCUS: MONEY-FREE MOMENTS

THE WHAT

Have you ever spent so much time on something that you started to dread having to go to or do that activity? You never want something you once loved to become a burden. The same goes for money. The amount of energy that you give to money can vary based on your desires, your lifestyle, and even your fears. During the path to achieve your financial goal, your brain may have become wired to think about your financial situation nonstop. You might be always thinking about how you can increase your income and where you can grow financially. But remember, it's okay to take a day or two off.

THE WHY

There will be times when everything else other than money seems far more critical. You will have days when your health, your loved ones, and your milestones outweigh your savings goal. Money can't be the driving factor in every decision you make in life.

THE HOW

There is more to life than a balanced budget. Learning to trust that you've built a solid foundation in saving for your future, preparing for emergencies, and the ability to afford exciting adventures is step one. Let's just focus on you this week.

What am I grateful for this week?

_____

_____

_____

What will be the most important thing I do this week?

_____

_____

_____

Who is someone who makes me happy?

_____

_____

_____

What can I do to show that person that I love them?

_____

_____

_____

What has been frustrating me that I can let go of?

_____

_____

_____

Three things that I love about myself:

1. _____

2. _____

3. _____

DAY 78

Date _____

CONNECT & REFLECT

Current mood (circle one): ☺ 😐 ☹ 😆 😄 😴

I FEEL _____

_____

_____

MONEY IS CURRENTLY _____

_____

_____

I WANT MONEY TO _____

_____

_____

WHAT WERE CHALLENGES THAT I FACED TODAY?

1. _____

_____

2. _____

_____

3. _____

_____

WHAT ARE SUCCESSES THAT I ENJOYED TODAY?

1. _____

_____

2. _____

_____

3. _____

WHERE DO I STAND?

☐ I need to get back on track to achieve my financial goal.

☐ I am on track with my financial goal.

TODAY'S EXPENSES

BUDGET CATEGORY	ITEM	COST
TOTAL		

TODAY'S INCOME

ITEM	AMOUNT
TOTAL	

DAY 79

Date _____

CONNECT & REFLECT

Current mood (circle one): 🙂 😐 🙁 😣 😆 😴

I FEEL _____

_____

_____

MONEY IS CURRENTLY _____

_____

_____

I WANT MONEY TO _____

_____

_____

WHAT WERE CHALLENGES THAT I FACED TODAY?

1. _____

_____

2. _____

_____

3. _____

_____

WHAT ARE SUCCESSES THAT I ENJOYED TODAY?

1. _____

_____

2. _____

_____

3. _____

☐ I need to get back on track to achieve my financial goal.

☐ I am on track with my financial goal.

TODAY'S EXPENSES

BUDGET CATEGORY	ITEM	COST
TOTAL		

TODAY'S INCOME

ITEM	AMOUNT
TOTAL	

DAY 80

Date _____

CONNECT & REFLECT

Current mood (circle one): ☺ ☻ ☹ 😆 😄 😴

I FEEL _____

_____

_____

MONEY IS CURRENTLY _____

_____

_____

I WANT MONEY TO _____

_____

_____

WHAT WERE CHALLENGES THAT I FACED TODAY?

1. _____

_____

2. _____

_____

3. _____

_____

WHAT ARE SUCCESSES THAT I ENJOYED TODAY?

1. _____

_____

2. _____

_____

3. _____

☐ I need to get back on track to achieve my financial goal.

☐ I am on track with my financial goal.

TODAY'S EXPENSES

BUDGET CATEGORY	ITEM	COST
TOTAL		

TODAY'S INCOME

ITEM	AMOUNT
TOTAL	

DAY 81

CONNECT & REFLECT

Current mood (circle one): ☺ 😐 ☹ 😣 😄 😴ᶻ

I FEEL _____

_____

_____

MONEY IS CURRENTLY _____

_____

_____

I WANT MONEY TO _____

_____

_____

WHAT WERE CHALLENGES THAT I FACED TODAY?

1. _____

_____

2. _____

_____

3. _____

_____

WHAT ARE SUCCESSES THAT I ENJOYED TODAY?

1. _____

_____

2. _____

_____

3. _____

☐ I need to get back on track to achieve my financial goal.

☐ I am on track with my financial goal.

TODAY'S EXPENSES

BUDGET CATEGORY	ITEM	COST
TOTAL		

TODAY'S INCOME

ITEM	AMOUNT
TOTAL	

DAY 82

Date _____

CONNECT & REFLECT

Current mood (circle one): 😊 😐 😟 😣 😄 😴

I FEEL _____

_____

_____

MONEY IS CURRENTLY _____

_____

_____

I WANT MONEY TO _____

_____

_____

WHAT WERE CHALLENGES THAT I FACED TODAY?

1. _____

_____

2. _____

_____

3. _____

_____

WHAT ARE SUCCESSES THAT I ENJOYED TODAY?

1. _____

_____

2. _____

_____

3. _____

☐ I need to get back on track to achieve my financial goal.

☐ I am on track with my financial goal.

TODAY'S EXPENSES

BUDGET CATEGORY	ITEM	COST
TOTAL		

TODAY'S INCOME

ITEM	AMOUNT
TOTAL	

DAY 83

Date _____

CONNECT & REFLECT

Current mood (circle one): ☺ 😐 ☹ 😫 😆 😴ᶻ

I FEEL _____

_____

_____

MONEY IS CURRENTLY _____

_____

_____

I WANT MONEY TO _____

_____

_____

WHAT WERE CHALLENGES THAT I FACED TODAY?

1. _____

_____

2. _____

_____

3. _____

_____

WHAT ARE SUCCESSES THAT I ENJOYED TODAY?

1. _____

_____

2. _____

_____

3. _____

☐ I need to get back on track to achieve my financial goal.

☐ I am on track with my financial goal.

TODAY'S EXPENSES

BUDGET CATEGORY	ITEM	COST
TOTAL		

TODAY'S INCOME

ITEM	AMOUNT
TOTAL	

DAY 84

Date _____

CONNECT & REFLECT

Current mood (circle one): ☺ 😐 ☹ 😣 😄 😴

I FEEL _____

_____

_____

MONEY IS CURRENTLY _____

_____

_____

I WANT MONEY TO _____

_____

_____

WHAT WERE CHALLENGES THAT I FACED TODAY?

1. _____

_____

2. _____

_____

3. _____

_____

WHAT ARE SUCCESSES THAT I ENJOYED TODAY?

1. _____

_____

2. _____

_____

3. _____

☐ I need to get back on track to achieve my financial goal.

☐ I am on track with my financial goal.

TODAY'S EXPENSES

BUDGET CATEGORY	ITEM	COST
TOTAL		

TODAY'S INCOME

ITEM	AMOUNT
TOTAL	

WEEKLY OUTLOOK

What could you improve on financially this week?

_____

_____

_____

_____

_____

_____

What was the best financial decision you made last week?

_____

_____

_____

_____

_____

Next week's motivations:

1. _____

_____

_____

_____

2. _____

_____

_____

_____

3. _____

_____

_____

_____

I WILL _____

_____

_____

_____

I WILL NOT _____

_____

_____

I AM _____

_____

_____

LAST PURCHASE: _____

_____

COST: _____

_____

THIS WEEK'S SAVINGS: _____

TOTAL MONEY SAVED/DEBT REPAID SO FAR: _____

_____

CURRENT WANT(S): _____

_____

CURRENT NEED(S): _____

_____

THIS WEEK'S FOCUS: MENTAL ACCOUNTING

THE WHAT

During this final stretch, it's time to muster up any additional income or money and put those resources toward your financial goal. One way to do this is by looking at how we treat our earnings. Unknowingly, we tend to treat the money we earn from different places differently. For instance, if you make money through your job, you tend to value those earnings in a different way than you would if someone were to give you the same amount for your birthday. You may put your paycheck toward essentials and savings, whereas you might spend a gift card more frivolously. This concept, discovered by Nobel Prize winner and economist Richard H. Thaler, is called mental accounting.

THE WHY

When we treat any money earned or received the same, we are more likely to put it toward our planned financial goals. Otherwise, our less-critical financial goals or habits may come first. You can't always take the emotional side of finance out of your day-to-day spending habits. However, we can control what we do when those emotional behaviors pop up by deciding how we'll manage our money before these moments arise.

THE HOW

If you struggle to treat all your money the same, it could be beneficial to set some boundaries or rules as to what you will do with every dollar you earn. For each type of earned money, decide whether to spend it for expenses, savings, or debt repayment based on the amount that you receive. For example, if the amount is under $100, you are free to spend on discretionary items. If the amount is over $100, allocate those funds toward debt or savings.

WHERE IS THE MONEY FROM?	WHERE WILL YOU ALLOCATE THE MONEY?
Full-time job	
A part-time job or side hustle	
Work bonus	
Gifts	
Winnings or prize money	
Tax refunds	
Found money	
Inheritance	
Loans or money repaid to you	
Sold belongings	
Other:	
Other:	
Other:	

Amounts under $_____ will be put toward discretionary spending.

Amounts above $_____ will be put toward expenses, debt, or savings.

DAY 85

CONNECT & REFLECT

Current mood (circle one): ☺ 😐 ☹ 😫 😄 😴

I FEEL _____

_____

_____

MONEY IS CURRENTLY _____

_____

_____

I WANT MONEY TO _____

_____

_____

WHAT WERE CHALLENGES THAT I FACED TODAY?

1. _____

_____

2. _____

_____

3. _____

_____

WHAT ARE SUCCESSES THAT I ENJOYED TODAY?

1. _____

_____

2. _____

_____

3. _____

☐ I need to get back on track to achieve my financial goal.

☐ I am on track with my financial goal.

TODAY'S EXPENSES

BUDGET CATEGORY	ITEM	COST
TOTAL		

TODAY'S INCOME

ITEM	AMOUNT
TOTAL	

DAY 86

Date _____

CONNECT & REFLECT

Current mood (circle one): 😊 😐 ☹️ 😫 😆 😴

I FEEL _____

_____

_____

MONEY IS CURRENTLY _____

_____

_____

I WANT MONEY TO _____

_____

_____

WHAT WERE CHALLENGES THAT I FACED TODAY?

1. _____

_____

2. _____

_____

3. _____

_____

WHAT ARE SUCCESSES THAT I ENJOYED TODAY?

1. _____

_____

2. _____

_____

3. _____

☐ I need to get back on track to achieve my financial goal.

☐ I am on track with my financial goal.

TODAY'S EXPENSES

BUDGET CATEGORY	ITEM	COST
TOTAL		

TODAY'S INCOME

ITEM	AMOUNT
TOTAL	

DAY 87

CONNECT & REFLECT

Current mood (circle one): 😊 😐 ☹️ 😆 😄 😴ᶻᶻ

I FEEL _____

_____

_____

MONEY IS CURRENTLY _____

_____

_____

I WANT MONEY TO _____

_____

_____

WHAT WERE CHALLENGES THAT I FACED TODAY?

1. _____

_____

2. _____

_____

3. _____

_____

WHAT ARE SUCCESSES THAT I ENJOYED TODAY?

1. _____

_____

2. _____

_____

3. _____

☐ I need to get back on track to achieve my financial goal.

☐ I am on track with my financial goal.

TODAY'S EXPENSES

BUDGET CATEGORY	ITEM	COST
TOTAL		

TODAY'S INCOME

ITEM	AMOUNT
TOTAL	

DAY 88

Date _____

CONNECT & REFLECT

Current mood (circle one): ☺ 😐 ☹ 😆 😋 😴

I FEEL _____

_____

_____

MONEY IS CURRENTLY _____

_____

_____

I WANT MONEY TO _____

_____

_____

WHAT WERE CHALLENGES THAT I FACED TODAY?

1. _____

_____

2. _____

_____

3. _____

_____

WHAT ARE SUCCESSES THAT I ENJOYED TODAY?

1. _____

_____

2. _____

_____

3. _____

☐ I need to get back on track to achieve my financial goal.

☐ I am on track with my financial goal.

TODAY'S EXPENSES

BUDGET CATEGORY	ITEM	COST
TOTAL		

TODAY'S INCOME

ITEM	AMOUNT
TOTAL	

DAY 89

CONNECT & REFLECT

Current mood (circle one): ☺ ☻ ☹ 😬 😆 😴

I FEEL _____

_____

_____

MONEY IS CURRENTLY _____

_____

_____

I WANT MONEY TO _____

_____

_____

WHAT WERE CHALLENGES THAT I FACED TODAY?

1. _____

_____

2. _____

_____

3. _____

_____

WHAT ARE SUCCESSES THAT I ENJOYED TODAY?

1. _____

_____

2. _____

_____

3. _____

☐ I need to get back on track to achieve my financial goal.

☐ I am on track with my financial goal.

TODAY'S EXPENSES

BUDGET CATEGORY	ITEM	COST
TOTAL		

TODAY'S INCOME

ITEM	AMOUNT
TOTAL	

DAY 90

CONNECT & REFLECT

Current mood (circle one):   ☺ 😐 😣 😬 😆 😴ᶻ

I FEEL _____

_____

_____

MONEY IS CURRENTLY _____

_____

_____

I WANT MONEY TO _____

_____

_____

WHAT WERE CHALLENGES THAT I FACED TODAY?

1. _____

_____

2. _____

_____

3. _____

_____

WHAT ARE SUCCESSES THAT I ENJOYED TODAY?

1. _____

_____

2. _____

_____

3. _____

☐ I need to get back on track to achieve my financial goal.

☐ I am on track with my financial goal.

TODAY'S EXPENSES

BUDGET CATEGORY	ITEM	COST
TOTAL		

TODAY'S INCOME

ITEM	AMOUNT
TOTAL	

DAY 91

CONNECT & REFLECT

Current mood (circle one): ☺ 😐 ☹ 😖 😄 😴

I FEEL _____

_____

_____

MONEY IS CURRENTLY _____

_____

_____

I WANT MONEY TO _____

_____

_____

WHAT WERE CHALLENGES THAT I FACED TODAY?

1. _____

_____

2. _____

_____

3. _____

_____

WHAT ARE SUCCESSES THAT I ENJOYED TODAY?

1. _____

_____

2. _____

_____

3. _____

☐ I need to get back on track to achieve my financial goal.

☐ I am on track with my financial goal.

TODAY'S EXPENSES

BUDGET CATEGORY	ITEM	COST
TOTAL		

TODAY'S INCOME

ITEM	AMOUNT
TOTAL	

WEEKLY OUTLOOK

What could you improve on financially this week?

_____

_____

_____

_____

_____

_____

What was the best financial decision you made last week?

_____

_____

_____

_____

_____

Next week's motivations:

1. _____

_____

_____

_____

2. _____

_____

_____

_____

3. _____

_____

_____

_____

I WILL _____

_____

_____

_____

I WILL NOT _____

_____

_____

I AM _____

_____

_____

LAST PURCHASE: _____

_____

COST: _____

_____

THIS WEEK'S SAVINGS: _____

TOTAL MONEY SAVED/DEBT REPAID SO FAR: _____

_____

CURRENT WANT(S): _____

_____

CURRENT NEED(S): _____

_____

THIS WEEK'S FOCUS: THE FINAL COUNTDOWN

THE WHAT

Can you believe we're already here? We've reached the final week of our journey together. It's time to do everything you can to close in on your deadline.

THE WHY

The closer you get to achieving your financial goal, it's likely you might need to do a little more to reach the finish line. If you're saving, there will be days when giving up extra expenses will free up a few extra dollars to help advance your financial success. If you're repaying debt, there might be a point when you know that adding an extra hundred dollars to your typical monthly payment means you're one or two weeks closer to freedom.

THE HOW

Before you make any plans for the week, don't. Now is the time to keep that entertainment budget sealed and get creative with whatever you've got in your fridge and pantry. Of course, we don't want you to feel suffocated, so don't feel as though you have to give up every little luxury in life; but if there is some way to make your goal seem that much closer, it might be worth it.

How much money do you need to save before you hit your financial goal?

_____

If possible, how much extra money can you allocate this week toward your goal?

BUDGETED ITEM	AMOUNT FOR BUDGETED ITEM	AMOUNT ALLOCATED FOR FINANCIAL GOAL	NEW AMOUNT FOR BUDGETED ITEM
ADDITIONAL AMOUNT FOR FINANCIAL GOAL			

DAY 92

Date _____

CONNECT & REFLECT

Current mood (circle one): 😊 😐 😣 😖 😄 😴

I FEEL _____

_____

_____

MONEY IS CURRENTLY _____

_____

_____

I WANT MONEY TO _____

_____

_____

WHAT WERE CHALLENGES THAT I FACED TODAY?

1. _____

_____

2. _____

_____

3. _____

_____

WHAT ARE SUCCESSES THAT I ENJOYED TODAY?

1. _____

_____

2. _____

_____

3. _____

☐ I need to get back on track to achieve my financial goal.

☐ I am on track with my financial goal.

TODAY'S EXPENSES

BUDGET CATEGORY	ITEM	COST
TOTAL		

TODAY'S INCOME

ITEM	AMOUNT
TOTAL	

DAY 93

Date _____

CONNECT & REFLECT

Current mood (circle one): ☺ 😐 ☹ 😣 😆 😴

I FEEL _____

_____

_____

MONEY IS CURRENTLY _____

_____

_____

I WANT MONEY TO _____

_____

_____

WHAT WERE CHALLENGES THAT I FACED TODAY?

1. _____

_____

2. _____

_____

3. _____

_____

WHAT ARE SUCCESSES THAT I ENJOYED TODAY?

1. _____

_____

2. _____

_____

3. _____

☐ I need to get back on track to achieve my financial goal.

☐ I am on track with my financial goal.

TODAY'S EXPENSES

BUDGET CATEGORY	ITEM	COST
TOTAL		

TODAY'S INCOME

ITEM	AMOUNT
TOTAL	

DAY 94

Date _____

CONNECT & REFLECT

Current mood (circle one): ☺ 😐 ☹ 😆 😄 😴

I FEEL _____

_____

_____

MONEY IS CURRENTLY _____

_____

_____

I WANT MONEY TO _____

_____

_____

WHAT WERE CHALLENGES THAT I FACED TODAY?

1. _____

_____

2. _____

_____

3. _____

_____

WHAT ARE SUCCESSES THAT I ENJOYED TODAY?

1. _____

_____

2. _____

_____

3. _____

☐ I need to get back on track to achieve my financial goal.

☐ I am on track with my financial goal.

TODAY'S EXPENSES

BUDGET CATEGORY	ITEM	COST
TOTAL		

TODAY'S INCOME

ITEM	AMOUNT
TOTAL	

DAY 95

CONNECT & REFLECT

Current mood (circle one): 🙂 😐 🙁 😣 😄 😴

I FEEL _____

_____

_____

MONEY IS CURRENTLY _____

_____

_____

I WANT MONEY TO _____

_____

_____

WHAT WERE CHALLENGES THAT I FACED TODAY?

1. _____

_____

2. _____

_____

3. _____

_____

WHAT ARE SUCCESSES THAT I ENJOYED TODAY?

1. _____

_____

2. _____

_____

3. _____

☐ I need to get back on track to achieve my financial goal.

☐ I am on track with my financial goal.

TODAY'S EXPENSES

BUDGET CATEGORY	ITEM	COST
TOTAL		

TODAY'S INCOME

ITEM	AMOUNT
TOTAL	

DAY 96

Date _____

CONNECT & REFLECT

Current mood (circle one): ☺ ☺ ☹ 😣 😄 😴

I FEEL _____

_____

_____

MONEY IS CURRENTLY _____

_____

_____

I WANT MONEY TO _____

_____

_____

WHAT WERE CHALLENGES THAT I FACED TODAY?

1. _____

_____

2. _____

_____

3. _____

_____

WHAT ARE SUCCESSES THAT I ENJOYED TODAY?

1. _____

_____

2. _____

_____

3. _____

☐ I need to get back on track to achieve my financial goal.

☐ I am on track with my financial goal.

TODAY'S EXPENSES

BUDGET CATEGORY	ITEM	COST
TOTAL		

TODAY'S INCOME

ITEM	AMOUNT
TOTAL	

DAY 97

CONNECT & REFLECT

Current mood (circle one): ☺ 😐 ☹ 😆 😂 😴ᶻ

I FEEL _____

_____

_____

MONEY IS CURRENTLY _____

_____

_____

I WANT MONEY TO _____

_____

_____

WHAT WERE CHALLENGES THAT I FACED TODAY?

1. _____

_____

2. _____

_____

3. _____

_____

WHAT ARE SUCCESSES THAT I ENJOYED TODAY?

1. _____

_____

2. _____

_____

3. _____

WHERE DO I STAND?

☐ I need to get back on track to achieve my financial goal.

☐ I am on track with my financial goal.

TODAY'S EXPENSES

BUDGET CATEGORY	ITEM	COST
TOTAL		

TODAY'S INCOME

ITEM	AMOUNT
TOTAL	

DAY 98

Date _____

CONNECT & REFLECT

Current mood (circle one): 🙂 😐 ☹️ 😬 😄 😴

I FEEL _____

_____

_____

MONEY IS CURRENTLY _____

_____

_____

I WANT MONEY TO _____

_____

_____

WHAT WERE CHALLENGES THAT I FACED TODAY?

1. _____

_____

2. _____

_____

3. _____

_____

WHAT ARE SUCCESSES THAT I ENJOYED TODAY?

1. _____

_____

2. _____

_____

3. _____

☐ I need to get back on track to achieve my financial goal.

☐ I am on track with my financial goal.

TODAY'S EXPENSES

BUDGET CATEGORY	ITEM	COST
TOTAL		

TODAY'S INCOME

ITEM	AMOUNT
TOTAL	

DAY 99

CONNECT & REFLECT

Current mood (circle one): ☺ 😐 🙁 😖 😂 😴

I FEEL _____

_____

_____

MONEY IS CURRENTLY _____

_____

_____

I WANT MONEY TO _____

_____

_____

WHAT WERE CHALLENGES THAT I FACED TODAY?

1. _____

_____

2. _____

_____

3. _____

_____

WHAT ARE SUCCESSES THAT I ENJOYED TODAY?

1. _____

_____

2. _____

_____

3. _____

☐ I need to get back on track to achieve my financial goal.

☐ I am on track with my financial goal.

TODAY'S EXPENSES

BUDGET CATEGORY	ITEM	COST
TOTAL		

TODAY'S INCOME

ITEM	AMOUNT
TOTAL	

DAY 100

CONNECT & REFLECT

Current mood (circle one): ☺ 😐 ☹ 😖 😂 😴ᶻ

I FEEL _____

_____

_____

MONEY IS CURRENTLY _____

_____

_____

I WANT MONEY TO _____

_____

_____

WHAT WERE CHALLENGES THAT I FACED TODAY?

1. _____

_____

2. _____

_____

3. _____

_____

WHAT ARE SUCCESSES THAT I ENJOYED TODAY?

1. _____

_____

2. _____

_____

3. _____

☐ I need to get back on track to achieve my financial goal.

☐ I am on track with my financial goal.

TODAY'S EXPENSES

BUDGET CATEGORY	ITEM	COST
TOTAL		

TODAY'S INCOME

ITEM	AMOUNT
TOTAL	

CONGRATULATIONS!

YOU MADE IT! NOW WHAT?

Over these 100 days, you have worked toward a goal. While this journey likely had its ups and downs, you truly pushed yourself beyond your comfort zone. You allowed yourself to put money toward things that were essential to your financial success. You have completely changed the course of your future just by deciding that you care about your money. Do you know how few people can say the same? Most will say it's reasonable to carry around debt or believe it's too hard to control their finances. You know that's not the reality.

At this point, you've learned many financial lessons and tackled many money challenges that used to stand in your way. Your new habits and skills are likely to continue to improve from here, but as with any new skill, you need to continually remind yourself and practice each of the lessons that you've learned to ensure that they become a part of your daily, weekly, and monthly routines. No one can control how you manage or spend your money other than you, which means that the best way to stay on top of things is by keeping up with the tools featured in this journal and referring back to old journal entries to see how far you have come in such a short amount of time. As you celebrate, it's helpful to reflect on what you've learned, how much you've grown, and where you will head from here. I hope that your financial journal has left you with newfound confidence in money management and made you feel hopeful about your financial future.

How will you celebrate?

_____

_____

_____

What did it feel like to reach Day 100?

_____

_____

_____

What were your greatest successes?

1. _____

2. _____

3. _____

What were your greatest challenges?

1. _____

2. _____

3. _____

Things that used to be financial struggles:

1. _____

2. _____

3. _____

Things that you're now capable of doing:

1. _____

2. _____

3. _____

What are three money affirmations that will help you build
a healthy financial future?

1. _____

_____

2. _____

_____

3. _____

_____

What is next for your money?

1. _____

_____

2. _____

_____

3. _____

_____

WRITE A FINAL CONGRATULATORY
NOTE TO YOURSELF.